indian recipes

indian recipes

bernard assiniwi

The Copp Clark Publishing Company
Toronto   Montreal   Vancouver

Cover and illustrations by Clayton Brascoupé.

© The Copp Clark Publishing Company 1972

All rights reserved. No part of the material covered by this copyright may be reproduced in any form or by any means (whether electronic, mechanical or photographic) for storage in retrieval systems, tapes, discs or for making multiple copies without the written permission of The Copp Clark Publishing Company.

Published in English with the
permission of Les Editions Leméac, Inc.

ISBN 0 7730 4005 6
Printed and bound in Canada

CONTENTS

Introduction / 1
Breads Bannock *Pakwejigan* / 5
Salads Hors-d'oeuvres Appetizers / 15
Soups *Nabos* / 23
Chowders *Kiniginige-Gigo* / 41
Meat Main Dishes / 47
Vegetable Main Dishes / 63
Seafood and Fish Main Dishes / 81
Desserts / 95
Beverages / 109
For the Outdoorsman / 117

INTRODUCTION

I have been working intermittently on this book for almost ten years, testing and selecting only those recipes which I particularly liked and wished to introduce to you.

In spite of all the efforts of governments and missionaries, the Indian way of life did evolve, and so did our tastes and recipes. We were familiar with the cauldron before the arrival of Jacques Cartier. And we had been using earthenware dishes and pots even before that time.

Frequently the recipes in this book call for unusual ingredients or ones that have been imported from other countries for more than 400 years. However, to facilitate the work of the modern housewife, many of the recipes have been adapted. I advise you to cook with natural spices, but ultimately, let your taste be your guide.

The traditional Indian spices are. . .

1) coltsfoot (the ashes of the burned leaves have a salty taste)
2) wild onions
3) wild leeks

4) wild thyme
5) wild mint
6) wood chips of cedar, maple, hickory and white ash
7) hemlock needles
8) juniper berries
9) pine cones
10) sumac fruits (and others you will find later in this book).

It might be interesting for the reader to know that the American Indians taught the civilized European to grow or at least to use twenty-nine different vegetables which were unknown on his own continent. In the southern part of our Indian land, we cultivated seventy-nine different vegetables:

9	edible seed plants
29	fruit trees and plants
28	vegetable plants
5	narcotic plants
3	fiber plants for the weaving of clothes
5	medical therapy plants

More than eighty-six varieties of corn were cultivated, but only twenty-one in the North. Some of the most important agricultural achievements made by North American Indians were very practical, such as the cultivation of cotton.

The recipes in this book are taken from different tribes in North America. An Algonquin recipe is titled with the Algonquin name, and when the source of the recipe is Iroquoian, the name remains in the Iroquoian language.

FLOUR

I recommend you use corn flour, or corn meal, but this can be replaced by wheat flour.

COOKING OIL
I suggest you use sunflower seed oil or corn oil for cooking or in your salads.

SALT
Sea salt or coltsfoot leaves (burned to ashes) should always be used as condiments with Indian foods. However, coarse salt is a very good substitute in the modern kitchen.

WARNING
The reader must recognize the fact that the author of this book is living in the twentieth century and, therefore, he has adapted the recipes for people living today. He doesn't guarantee their success.

Have a good meal. . . . the Indian way.
Ni't'chawama
Bernard Assiniwi

BREADS
Bannock
Pakwejigan

Bannock is cooked in the embers or in the hot ashes.

Bannock, also called bannick or Indian bread, is called "pakwejigan" by my people. It is the easiest bread to make, tastes delicious and keeps well without becoming mouldy. For variation, add raisins, blueberries or raspberries. Wild mint tea, raspberry jam and fresh pakwejigan at breakfast have no equal...for an Indian.

Epangishimog Pakwejigan
   Shuswap Bannock   7
Inagami-Pakwejigan
   Soft Bread   8
Anish-Nah-Be Pakwejigan
   The Real Indian Bread   9
Pakwejigan
   Bread   10
Missiiagan-Pakwejigan
   Sunflower Seed Bannock   11
Pagan-Pakwejigan
   Wild Nut Bannock   12
Gigo-Pakwejigan
   Fish Bannock   13

EPANGISHIMOG PAKWEJIGAN
SHUSWAP BANNOCK

Tribe: Shuswap
Source: Mrs. Simon Baker, Cappilano Indian Reserve, North Vancouver, B.C.

---

    3   cups of all purpose flour
    1   tablespoon of baking powder
    1 1/2 teaspoons of sea salt
    1 1/2 cups of water
    1   cup of blueberries

a) Mix the dry ingredients together, then add the water quickly and continue to stir.
b) Spread on a pie plate and put in the oven at 425°F, for 20 minutes.
c) Cut in pieces and serve cold or hot.

Excellent with mint tea. Serves eight persons.

This recipe was given to me by Mrs. Baker while we were attending the Chilliwack War Canoe Races at Chilliwack Lake, B.C. in the summer of 1967.

INAGAMI-PAKWEJIGAN
SOFT BREAD

Tribe: Ojibway
Source: Martin Assiniwe, Birch Island Reserve, Ontario

---

    1 3/4 cups of water
    2/3 cup of white corn flour
    3/4 teaspoon of sea salt
    Some butter and crushed sunflower seeds

a) Bring water to the boil while you mix together the flour and the salt.
b) Pour boiling water on the dry ingredients while stirring and continue to stir until mixture becomes thick and uniform.
c) Serve in a bowl topped with fresh butter and sunflower seeds.

It's delicious! Serves three to six persons.

ANISH-NAH-BE PAKWEJIGAN
THE REAL INDIAN BREAD

Tribe: Odawa and Ojibway
Source: Georgina King, Wikwimikong Reserve,
Manitoulin Island, Ontario

Make some soft dough using the recipe on the facing page.

    2/3 cup of animal fat or sunflower seed oil
    1/2 cup of blueberries or raisins

a) When the soft dough is at room temperature, mix in the blueberries and put the dough into a bowl and chill to thicken.
b) When firm, cut it in ½ inch slices, and fry until a golden color.
c) Serve hot with melted butter and honey or maple syrup.

Makes three to five servings.

PAKWEJIGAN
BREAD

Tribes: Odawa, Ojibway, Algonquin, Montagnais and Cree
Source: Georgina King, Odawa Wikwimikong Indian Reserve, Manitoulin Island, Ontario

---

    1 cup of all purpose flour
    1/4 teaspoon of sea salt
    1/2 teaspoon of baking powder
    3 tablespoons of porcupine fat or sunflower seed oil
    1/3 cup of water
    1/4 cup of shortening or corn oil

a) Mix together the dry ingredients and add the porcupine fat or sunflower seed oil; mix well.
b) Add the water and knead well.
c) Heat the shortening or the oil in a frying pan.
d) Spread the bread in it, and fry until golden brown. Serve hot.

This is the most common bannock recipe. Serves three hungry hunters.

MISSIIAGAN-PAKWEJIGAN
SUNFLOWER SEED BANNOCK

Tribe: Mohawk
Source: Sarah Goodleaf, Caughnawaga Indian Reserve, Quebec

---

      3 1/4 cups of sunflower seeds
      3 1/4 cups of water
      2 1/2 teaspoons of sea salt or coltsfoot leaves salt
      6 tablespoons of corn flour
      2/3 cup of corn oil or animal fat

a) 1. Put the sunflower seeds, water and salt in a saucepan, cover and let simmer for 1½ hours.
   2. When well cooked, crush the seeds to make a paste.
b) Add the corn flour, one tablespoon at a time to thicken and work it with your hands; cool a little.
c) Make small, flat "pancakes" of approximately 5 inches in diameter.
d) Heat the oil, and fry the pieces on both sides. Add more oil if necessary. Drain well, and try it.

Makes eighteen small loaves.

PAGAN-PAKWEJIGAN
WILD NUT BANNOCK

Tribe: Algonquin
Source: Mary Commanda, Rivière Desert Reserve, Maniwaki, Quebec

---

    3/4 pound of wild hazelnuts (crushed)
    3 cups of water
    2/3 cup of corn flour
    1 1/3 teaspoons of sea salt or coltsfoot leaves salt
    1 cup frying oil (corn or sunflower seed oil)

a) Boil the nuts in water, stirring occasionally until they turn to a mash.
b) Mix together the flour and salt and add the mashed nuts; let mixture thicken for 30 minutes.
c) Heat the oil in a thick saucepan. Drop the mixture, one tablespoon at a time, in the hot oil. Fry both sides until golden brown.

Serve like bread. Makes fifteen small cakes.

GIGO-PAKWEJIGAN
FISH BANNOCK

Tribe: Maleseet
Source: Mrs. Charles Paul, Maleseet Reserve, Tobique, N.B.

    1/2 pound of fresh boiled fish with its juice
    1/4 cup of corn flour
    1/3 cup of milk
    1 egg (lightly beaten)

a) Mix all ingredients.
b) Bake in an oven at 350°F for 30 minutes.

Serve hot or cold. Makes three to five servings.

SALADS
HORS-D'OEUVRES
APPETIZERS

Only one salad recipe is given in this section because the ingredients for most Indian salads are not available on the market and picking their ingredients in the woods by inexperienced persons could bring about some accidents. However, my companion book, Survival in the Bush, *details some edible wilds that can be picked without any danger. It will be up to you to create your own salads.*

These so-called "hors-d'oeuvres" used to be full meals for our people. Smoked salmon and caviar were (and still are) delicacies eaten with bread for breakfast by the West Coast Indians. Smoked eel soup was a favourite dish for the Mohawk Indians, from the month of April to the end of June. Clams are still a delicacy for the Micmac Indians of the eastern coast, and calves brain takes the place of buffalo brain in the Blackfoot and Cree diets nowadays.

Ojawashkwawegad
   Wild Green Salad   17
Gigo
   Fish Delight   18
Gigo-Wawanons
   Smoked Salmon and Salmon Caviar   19
Bimisi
   Smoked Eel, Mohawk Style   20
Kitchigami-Midjim
   Clams, Micmac Style   21
Nindib
   Fried Brain   22

OJAWASHKWAWEGAD
WILD GREEN SALAD

Tribe: Algonquin
Source: Mrs. Mary Commanda, Rivière Desert Reserve, Maniwaki, Quebec

---

Salad

    1 cup of wild onions or wild leeks, well chopped
    1 quart or more of fresh wild watercress
    1/4 cup of sheep or wood sorrel (sour leaves)
    1 1/2 cups of fresh spring dandelion leaves

Salad Dressing

    1/3 cup of salad oil (preferably sunflower seed oil)
    1/3 cup of cider vinegar
    3 tablespoons of natural honey or birch sap or maple sap
    3/4 teaspoon of vegetable salt or coltsfoot leaves salt
    1/4 teaspoon of black pepper

You can make many variations of this salad using the wild, edible ingredients mentioned in my companion book, Survival in the Bush.

GIGO
FISH DELIGHT

Tribe: Micmac
Source: Mrs. Thomas Gédéon, Restigouche Reserve, Quebec

---

    3 pounds of fresh fish (walleye, pike, bass, etc.)
    1 quart of yellow waterlily roots (well washed and peeled), diced
    2 cups of water
    2 tablespoons of butter
    1 teaspoon of sea salt
  1/3 teaspoon of black pepper
    1 quart of fat or cooking oil (corn or sunflower seed oil)

a) Put the waterlily roots, fish and water in a pot with a close-fitting cover and boil for 35 minutes.
b) When cooked, put the fish and waterlily roots on absorbent paper to drain, then mash them.
c) Add the melted butter, salt and pepper.
d) Roll in small balls 2 or 3 inches in diameter.
e) Heat the oil in a deep saucepan until the oil reaches approx. 400°F.
f) Drop the balls into the hot fat and fry until golden brown.

Serve hot. Serves eight persons.

GIGO-WAWANONS
SMOKED SALMON AND SALMON CAVIAR

Tribe: Shuswap
Source: Mrs. Simon Baker, Cappilano Indian Reserve, North Vancouver, B.C.

1/3 pound smoked salmon, thinly sliced
6 ounces of salmon caviar
2 wild onions or 4 shallots, finely chopped

You will also need some of the bannock bread called "Epangishimog Pakwejigan."

a) Lay the salmon slices on the bannock, and cover it with the caviar.
b) Cover this with the chopped wild onions.
c) Cut into small pieces and eat as is or put them under the broiler to brown.

Both ways are delicious! Serves eight persons.

BIMISI
SMOKED EEL, MOHAWK STYLE

Tribe: Mohawk
Source: Peter Diome (Chief), Caughnawaga Indian Reserve, Quebec

---

Approximately 2 pounds of smoked eel (cut it into 2 inch pieces, but take the skin off first)
4 big cattail roots or great burdock roots (washed and peeled)
6 wild onions or 8 shallots with tops
8 cups of water
1/4 teaspoon of black pepper, freshly ground

a) Simmer all the ingredients in a large iron pot for 1 or 2 hours or until the cattail roots are tender.
b) Skim the fat from the surface and serve hot.

Makes eight servings.

KITCHIGAMI-MIDJIM
CLAMS, MICMAC STYLE

Tribe: Micmac
Source: Mrs. Thomas Gédéon, Restigouche Reserve, Quebec

---

    2 1/2 dozen big, juicy clams in their shells
    2 cups of water
    1/2 cup of butter or margarine
    3 tablespoons of wild watercress, finely chopped (or dandelions or black mustard)

a) Clean the clams with a brush in cold water.
b) Place them on a stand in a large pot, add water and cover tightly.
c) Let it boil for 15 or 20 minutes.
d) In another saucepan, melt the butter and mix in the chopped watercress to make a sauce.
e) Place the sauce in a small dish and arrange the clams on a platter around it.

Makes four to six servings.

NINDIB
FRIED BRAIN

Tribe: Blackfoot
Source: Mrs. Joe Bear-Robe, Blackfoot Indian Reserve, Cluny, Alberta

---

- 2 wild duck eggs (or chicken eggs)
- 3 tablespoons of corn flour
- 3/4 teaspoon of sea salt or vegetable salt
- 1/4 teaspoon of pepper
- 2 pounds of fresh moose, deer or calf brain, cut into bite-sized pieces
- 4 tablespoons of animal fat or corn oil for frying

a) Beat the eggs with the corn flour, salt and pepper.
b) Add the brain and mix well.
c) Heat the fat or oil, and sauté the brain in it for about 15 minutes.

Serve hot. Serves three cowboys.

SOUPS
Nabos

An earthenware pot for cooking soup. The handle allows the cook to stir the soup without leaning over the steam and getting burnt.

Soups are definitely the basis of Indian cooking in Canada. From corn to beans, from nuts to pumpkins, from oysters to mushrooms — everything was used to make soups.

Paganens	
Algonquin Wild Nut Soup	25
Miskwessabo	
Micmac Oyster Soup	26
Ogwissimanabo	
Yellow Squash Soup	27
Missabigonabo	
Pumpkin Soup	28
Miskodissimin-Opinabo	
Pea, Bean and Potato Soup	29
Kitchi-Jigagamanj-Nabo	
Wild Onion Soup	30
Nadowe-Nabo	
Iroquoian Soup	31
Bassitagan	
Sun Soup	32
Abnakisnabo	
Abnakis Soup	33
Nadowessabo	
Huron Soup	34
Anissabo	
Pea Soup Cree Style	35
Pagwadji-Mitig-Nabo	
Black Mustard and Fish Soup	36
Gigonassigan-Abo	
Smoked Salmon Soup	37
Kitchigami-Nabo	
Soup from the Sea	38

PAGANENS
ALGONQUIN WILD NUT SOUP

Tribe: Algonquin
Source: Mary Commanda, Rivière Desert Reserve, Maniwaki, Quebec

---

    24 ounces of wild hazelnuts, crushed
    1 beef tail or 2 cubes of beef consommé
    6 wild onions or 6 shallots with tops
    3 tablespoons of parsley, finely chopped
    6 cups of water
    1 teaspoon of vegetable salt
    1/4 teaspoon of black pepper

Place all the ingredients in a large iron pot and simmer slowly on medium heat for 1½ hours, stirring occasionally.

This is a traditional fall soup for Algonquin Indians. Serves six hunters.

MISKWESSABO
MICMAC OYSTER SOUP

Tribe: Micmac
Source: Mrs. Thomas Gédéon, Restigouche Reserve, Quebec

---

    30 big oysters with their juice
    1/3 cup of butter
    2 1/2 cups of milk
    1/4 cup corn flour or wheat flour
    1/2 teaspoon of sea salt
    1/4 teaspoon of black pepper
    2 leaves of wild mint

a) Place oysters, their juice and the butter in a saucepan.
b) Mix 1/4 cup of milk with the flour; add the remaining milk and mix with the oysters.
c) Add mint leaves.
d) Heat slowly, stirring continuously for 25 minutes.
e) Season to your taste and serve.

Serves six persons.

This recipe was given to Mrs. Gédéon by Suzanne Matallic of Cape Breton Island.

OGWISSIMANABO
YELLOW SQUASH SOUP

Tribe: Tuscarora
Source: Many Jamieson, Six-Nations Reserve, Ohsweken, Ontario

---

    1   medium-sized yellow squash, cut into pieces
    2   wild onions or 4 shallots with tops (chopped)
    1   quart of water (more or less, according to size of squash)
    2   tablespoons of natural honey
    4 to 6 1/2 inch slices of cucumber
    1   tablespoon of vegetable salt or coltsfoot leaves salt
    1/4 teaspoon of black pepper

a) Place the squash, wild onions, water and honey in a large cauldron and simmer 40 minutes until the squash is tender; then add the cucumbers.
b) Put everything in a large bowl and mash until it forms a thick, creamy paste (use a blender if you have one).
c) Put the mixture into the cauldron and season with salt and pepper; simmer 5 or 10 minutes.

Serve hot. Makes six servings.

MISSABIGONABO
PUMPKIN SOUP

Tribe: Tuscarora
Source: Many Jamieson, Six-Nations Reserve, Ohsweken, Ontario

---

    2   pounds (or 30 liquid ounces) of boiled and mashed pumpkin
    1   quart of milk (40 ounces)
    3   tablespoons of butter or margarine
    3   tablespoons of natural honey
    3   tablespoons of maple sugar or brown sugar
    1/2 teaspoon of wild thyme or commercial thyme
    1   pinch of black pepper
    1/4 teaspoon of vegetable salt or coltsfoot leaves salt

a) Heat the pumpkin mash, milk, butter and honey, stirring gently.
b) Mix the maple sugar, thyme, pepper and salt and pour into the mash while stirring.
c) Simmer 15 to 20 minutes, do not boil.

Serve hot. Makes ten to twelve servings.

MISKODISSIMIN-OPINABO
PEA, BEAN AND POTATO SOUP

Tribe: Abnakis
Source: Jean Hoff, Odanak-Abnakis Reserve, Quebec

    1/2 pound of dried soup peas
    1/2 pound of black beans
    4 big potatoes
    4 tablespoons of butter
    4 teaspoons of vegetable salt or coltsfoot leaves salt
    1/2 teaspoon of black pepper
    1/2 cup of chopped wild onions or shallots with tops

a) Wash, soak and cook peas and beans as indicated in package directions; retain the cooking water.
b) Cook the potatoes and keep the cooking water.
c) Measure cooking water from beans and potatoes to 8 cups; if not enough, add fresh water. Put in a soup pot.
d) Crush the peas and beans with potatoes and add to the liquid, with all other ingredients.
e) Simmer slowly for one hour.

Serve hot. Makes ten servings.

KITCHI-JIGAGAMANJ-NABO
WILD ONION SOUP

Tribe: Algonquin
Source: Mary Commanda, Rivière Desert Reserve, Maniwaki, Quebec

---

    2   pounds of wild onions with lower part of tops (or 2 1/2 pounds of shallots with tops)
    8   cups of water
    3/4 cup of wild watercress
    1 1/2 teaspoons of coltsfoot leaves salt or sea salt
    1/4 teaspoon of freshly ground green pepper

a) Finely chop the wild onions.
b) Put all the ingredients into soup pot and simmer 35 to 45 minutes.
c) Season with salt and pepper and serve.

Makes six servings.

NADOWE-NABO
IROQUOIAN SOUP

Tribe: Tuscarora
Source: Many Jamieson, Six-Nations Reserve, Ohsweken, Ontario

---

    5 big mushrooms, thinly sliced
    3 cups of beef consommé (canned)
    3 tablespoons of yellow corn flour
    3 tablespoons of wild watercress, finely chopped
    1 clove of garlic or 3 wild onions with lower part of tops
  1/4 teaspoon of wild or domestic thyme
    1 medium onion, finely chopped
    1 pinch of black pepper
  1/2 teaspoon of vegetable salt
    1 pound of walleye fillets or any fresh water white fish meat
    1 pound of cooked lima beans
    1 little glass of "p'tit caribou" (see the recipe in this book under "Beverages")

a) Place mushrooms, consommé, corn flour, watercress, garlic, thyme, onion, wild onions, salt and pepper in a large kettle; simmer uncovered for 10 to 12 minutes.

b) Add the fish fillets, the beans and the "p'tit caribou" and simmer 20 minutes stirring occasionally.

Serve hot. Makes four to six servings.
Le p'tit caribou is 1 part sherry and 1 part white alcohol.

BASSITAGAN
SUN SOUP

Tribe: Tuscarora
Source: Many Jamieson, Six-Nations Indian Reserve, Ohsweken, Ontario

---

    2 1/2 cups of sunflower seeds (without the shells)
    6 wild onions or 8 shallots with tops
    6 cups of thick chicken broth
    1 teaspoon of sea salt

Put all the ingredients in a large pot and simmer for one hour.

Serve hot. Makes six servings.

ABNAKISNABO
ABNAKIS SOUP

Tribe: Abnakis
Source: Eighteenth-century tradition

>40 ounces of tomatoes, cooked and crushed
>2 cups of milk
>1/4 teaspoon of onion salt
>1 pound of corn
>pepper to taste

Put all ingredients together in a kettle and bring to a boil, but only for five minutes.
You can replace the fresh tomatoes with preserved cream of tomatoes, but you lose much of the flavour.

Makes six servings.

The tomato was first imported in our country from Virginia. The Abnakis came from New England in 1701 and were known as extensive travellers. They loved tomatoes and many recipes including the tomato come from them.

NADOWESSABO
HURON SOUP

Tribe: Huron-Wendat
Source: Fr. Sagard's Memoirs

New method
    4 slices of bacon
    1/2 cup of wild onions or domestic onions, finely chopped
    2 cups of chicken broth or 2 cubes of concentrated chicken broth dissolved in 2 cups of boiling water
    3/4 teaspoon of celery salt or vegetable salt
    1 cup of mashed potatoes
    2 1/2 cups of creamed corn
    1 1/2 cups evaporated milk or table cream

a) Brown the bacon with the wild onions, slowly.
b) Heat the chicken broth and add the bacon and onions to it, along with the celery salt and mashed potatoes.
c) Add the creamed corn and the milk or cream.
d) Stir slowly and heat, never boil; add water if too thick.

Originally this recipe was...
    4 slices of beaver sides (along the ribs)
    10 wild onions with tops
    1 quart of goose broth
    celery salt and big grains of pepper
    1/2 cup of corn meal (to replace potatoes)
    3 cobs of corn
    1 1/2 cups of ewe's milk

ANISSABO
PEA SOUP CREE STYLE

Tribe: Cree
Source: My Father, Léonidas Assiniwi

---

   2 cups of dried peas (soak them for 12 hours)
20 ounces of hominy (blown corn)
   1 cup of celery leaves (fresh) or 2 pinches of thyme
salt, pepper and savory
16 cups of water

When the soaking peas are soft, put them in a cauldron with all the other ingredients and simmer until the peas are tender and firm. I prefer to add the hominy only when the peas are well cooked. When this soup is thick, it is a meal by itself.

PAGWADJI-MITIG-NABO
BLACK MUSTARD AND FISH SOUP

Tribe: Cree (Tête de Boule)
Source: Paul Awashish, Manoanne Reserve, Quebec

---

    4 roots of great burdock or 4 small potatoes
    4 wild onions or 2 small onions, cut in half
    1 1/2 quarts of water
    6 black peppercorns
    1 pound of black mustard leaves (see companion book, *Survival in the Bush*)
    1 1/2 pounds of white fish meat
  10 wild mint leaves
    2 teaspoons of vegetable salt or sea salt

a) Place great burdock roots (or potatoes), wild onions, water, pepper in a large saucepan and bring to boiling point.
b) Lower heat and simmer 50 to 60 minutes.
c) Reduce the roots to small pieces by mashing them.
d) Add the fresh fish meat and simmer 10 more minutes, breaking the meat into small pieces.
e) Stir and add the black mustard leaves, wild mint and salt; simmer 5 more minutes.

Serve as a soup or pass through a strainer and serve the juice as a consommé. Serves eight to ten persons.

GIGONASSIGAN-ABO
SMOKED SALMON SOUP

Tribe: Seshelt
Source: Mrs. George Clutesi,
Port Alberni, B.C.

---

    1 pound of smoked salmon, sliced
    32 ounces of water
    1/4 teaspoon of pepper
    3/4 cup of black mustard leaves

a) Break the salmon up into small pieces and place in a saucepan with water and pepper; simmer slowly, stirring occasionally for 15 minutes.
b) Add the black mustard leaves and simmer another 5 minutes.

Serve hot.

KITCHIGAMI-NABO
SOUP FROM THE SEA

Tribe: Micmac
Source: George Menecho,
Eel River, N.B.

---

   1 3/4 pounds of small shrimps (fresh)
   4 tablespoons of corn oil
   6 wild onions finely chopped or 2 large onions
   1 pound of fish heads, (cod fish heads or white fish heads)
   1 teaspoon of shallot tops, minced
   2 big tomatoes, peeled and chopped in small pieces
   2 teaspoons of sea salt
1/2 teaspoon of fresh black pepper
   2 quarts of water (80 ounces)
   3 potatoes, peeled and diced
   4 potatoes, cut in half
1/2 cup of wild rice or long grain brown rice
   1 pound of green peas or lima beans
   3 cobs of corn, cut in thirds
   3 eggs
10 ounces of milk
   2 tablespoons of fresh watercress, minced
1/3 teaspoon of thyme

a) Shell the shrimps and clean them by removing the intestinal vein along the back (keep the shells).
b) In a large saucepan, heat the oil on medium heat and brown the wild onions, the shrimp shells, the fish heads

and the minced wild onion tops.
c) Reduce heat and cook for 8 minutes, stirring occasionally.
d) Add the tomatoes, thyme, salt and pepper and cook for 4 minutes.
e) Add the water, diced potatoes and fry for 30 minutes.
f) Place everything in a strainer so as to retain solid elements as much as possible.
g) Put this mash back into the saucepan, bring to a boil, add the potatoes cut in half and the wild rice.
h) Cover, reduce heat and simmer for 30 minutes.
i) When potatoes are cooked, add the green peas and corn and cook for 5 minutes; then add shrimps and cook until they turn to a pink color.
j) Meanwhile, beat the eggs and pour them into the soup, stirring all the time as you pour the liquid.
k) Add the milk, and heat a little; garnish with watercress or parsley.

Serves four people.

CHOWDERS
Kiniginige-Gigo

Chowders should be cooked slowly. They are made of seafood and fish, but vegetables also have their place.

Chowders are among the finest soups one can taste. Only three were selected for this book as they seemed to be the most representative of the taste and culture of the fishermen Indians of the Atlantic and Pacific coasts, as well as of the inland fishermen, the Iroquois. Of course, we did not use cream before the Europeans brought cows to North America some four hundred years ago. But four hundred years might be a sufficient length of time for this ingredient to be part of our culture. . .don't you think?

    Micmac Kiniginige
        Micmac Chowder   43
    Nadowe-Kiniginige
        Iroquois Chowder   44
    Gigo-Kiniginige
        Seshelt Chowder   46

MICMAC KINIGINIGE
MICMAC CHOWDER

Tribe: Micmac
Source: Mrs. Thomas Gédéon, Restigouche Reserve, Quebec

---

  2 slices of lean pork, cut in *julienne* strips
  6 wild onions or 8 shallots
30 clams without the shells
  3 tablespoons of butter
  3 tablespoons of corn flour (white)
  3 cups of water
  4 diced cattail roots (or potatoes)
  1 teaspoon of sea salt
1/8 teaspoon of freshly ground pepper
1/4 cup of watercress, finely chopped

a) Cook the pork and add the wild onions; sauté it all.
b) Open the clams, keep the juice and add the clams to the pork and onions, then mix the flour and butter, heat and stir for two minutes.
c) Add the juice from the clams and the water, the diced cattail roots, salt and pepper.
d) Simmer covered for 2 hours, stirring occasionally.
e) When the chowder is ready, add the watercress, simmer 5 minutes and serve hot.

Makes eight servings.

NADOWE-KINIGINIGE
IROQUOIS CHOWDER

Tribe: Mohawk
Source: Mrs. Margaret Deer, Caughnawaga Indian Reserve, Quebec

---

- 1 pound of fish fillets (pike, bass, perch)
- 1 cup of water
- 6 minced wild onions or one big onion
- 3 tablespoons of melted butter
- 1 tablespoon of corn flour
- 1 cup of diced potatoes
- 1/2 cup of finely chopped celery
- 1/4 teaspoon of black pepper, freshly ground
- 3 cups of milk, scalded
- 3/4 cup of sweet cream
- 1/2 cup of sour cream (you can make it by adding the juice of a lemon)
- 1 handful of fresh parsley, finely chopped
- 1 pinch of thyme
- 1 bay leaf
- 1 1/2 teaspoons of sea salt

a) Poach the fish fillets for about 5 minutes, strain and keep the broth. Cook the wild onions in butter for 5 minutes, add the flour gradually, while stirring. Cook until the mixture is smooth, add the potatoes, celery, bay leaf, salt and pepper. Simmer on low heat 15 minutes until the potatoes are tender.

b) Mix together the heated milk, sweet cream and sour cream and beat well.
c) Pour over the potato mixture and add the fish while stirring.
d) Heat on medium heat 5 to 10 minutes. Do not boil.
e) Take out the bay leaf and garnish with parsley.

Serves eight persons.

GIGO-KINIGINIGE
SESHELT CHOWDER

Tribe: Seshelt
Source: Mrs. George Clutesi,
Port Alberni, B.C.

---

    4 big cattail roots, roasted and diced
    5 cups of water
    1 1/2 pounds of roughly cut salmon (fresh)
    1/4 teaspoon of fresh pepper
    2 teaspoons of sea salt

a) Simmer the cattail roots for 40 minutes.
b) Add the other ingredients and simmer 10 more minutes.

Serve hot. Makes six servings.

MEAT MAIN DISHES

Pag-Wadjawessi
   Six-Game Paté   49
Wajashk
   Muskrats with Bacon   51
Makwa-Wiiass
   Bear Rump Roast   52
Amik-Wiiass
   Beaver   53
Inini-Jishib
   Stuffed Duck   54
Wewe
   Roasted Goose   56
Pamaakwe or Bine
   Partridge or Grouse Algonquin Style   58
Wabos-Wiiass
   Rabbit Stew   59
Mons-Ode-Ima
   Moose Heart   60
Kag
   Porcupine   61

PAG-WADJAWESSI
SIX-GAME PATE

This dish is Indian, although the Québecois living in the lower St. Lawrence Region adopted it centuries ago. In the Lac St. Jean area, potatoes are added to it. The Micmac make this dish with fish and sea food.

Spices

      cloves, cinnamon, salt, pepper, wild onions (3)

You need the following game meat...

    2 wild rabbits (boneless)
    2 wild partridges
    1 1/2 pounds of deer meat or moose meat, diced in 1 1/2 to 2 inch pieces
    1 pound of beaver meat (diced)
    2 wild ducks (the big blacks)

If you do not have wild game, you can make the dish with...

    1 domestic rabbit (boneless)
    2 pounds of chicken meat (boneless)
    1 pound of beef meat, diced in 1 1/2 to 2 inch pieces
    1 pound of veal, diced in 1 1/2 to 2 inch pieces
    1 1/2 pounds of pork, diced in 1 1/2 to 2 inch pieces

a) You need a big cast iron pot. Grease the inside.
b) Make a pie crust of corn or wheat flour, and cover the bottom and sides of the pot, letting the crust extend about 2 inches.
c) Put one row of game meat around the bottom, leaving a 2 inch hole in the center, then add alternate rows of crust and meat, always keeping the hole in the center. For each row, add a bit of each spice.
d) Fill the hole with water and cover it all with a top crust. Cover the pot and put it in the oven at 250°F-300°F for about 8 hours.
e) For the last hour of cooking, uncover about 2½ inches so the crust will brown.

Serves ten persons.

WAJASHK
MUSKRATS WITH BACON

Tribe: Algonquin
Source: Tradition from the Rivière Desert Reserve, Maniwaki, Quebec

---

    12 wild onions or 15 shallots
    4 big muskrats, washed and cleaned
    8 slices of fat bacon
    1 lemon
    salt, pepper, thyme or wild mint
    4 wild onions or 8 shallots
    2 cups of water
    1 1/2 cups of wild rice, cooked and cooled
    1/2 cup of "p'tit caribou" (see the recipe in "Beverages")

a) In a large saucepan, boil the 12 wild onions, then drop the 4 muskrats in it for 60 seconds only.
b) Place two strips of bacon on each muskrat to cover them.
c) Sprinkle with salt, pepper, thyme or mint.
d) Inside each muskrat put one wild onion, finely chopped.
e) Squeeze the lemon and sprinkle the juice over the muskrats.
f) Sprinkle the "p'tit caribou" over the meat.
g) Put the muskrats on a dripping pan and place it in the oven at 300°F, sprinkling frequently with water. Cook for 30 minutes to 1 hour.
h) Serve on a bed of wild rice mixed with wild onions, finely chopped.

Serves four persons.

MAKWA-WIIASS
BEAR RUMP ROAST

Tribe: Cree
Source: Bernard Assiniwi, Rivière Desert Reserve, Maniwaki, Quebec

---

    1 5-pound rump roast of young bear (boneless)
    8 wild onions or 12 shallots
    1 pound of lima beans (cooked)
    a lump of butter the size of an egg
    1 cup of maple syrup
    2 cups of water or 1 cup of red wine
    salt, pepper and thyme
    watercress for garnishing

a) Boil water in a very large iron pot and add the bear rump for 5 minutes to remove some of the fat.
b) Make small holes in the meat and insert the wild onions.
c) Sprinkle salt, pepper and thyme over the meat and brown it all over in butter, then place it in a dripping pan, with water and wine, and put it in the oven at 275°F for approximately 4 hours, sprinkling frequently with water.
d) Pour maple syrup over the rump roast and put it back in the oven for 2 more hours at 275°F.
e) Serve on a bed of lima beans, decorated with fresh watercress.

The cooking time can vary depending on the age of the animal, so don't take the time suggested here as absolute.

AMIK-WIIASS
BEAVER

Tribe: Algonquin
Source: Mary Commanda, Rivière Desert Reserve, Maniwaki, Quebec

---

    1/2 a beaver (about 10 pounds — the front part has a better taste)
    10 wild onions or 4 big onions
    8 carrots
    a lump of butter the size of an egg
    8 Jerusalem artichoke roots (or 8 medium potatoes)
    salt, pepper to taste, one pinch of ground cloves and one pinch of cinnamon
    water to cook the meat

a) In a cast iron pot, boil the beaver with the wild onions for about 30 minutes. Take the beaver out and place it in a dripping pan.
b) Arrange the carrots and the Jerusalem artichokes around the beaver. Add the salt, pepper, ground cloves and cinnamon to a small amount of water and pour this mixture into the bottom of the pan.
c) Baste meat with the beaver drippings and juice, 4 or 5 times during the 3 to 4 hours of cooking in the oven at 300°F.

Serve with vegetables and bannock. If you like alcohol, you can baste the meat with "p'tit caribou."

ININI-JISHIB
STUFFED DUCK

Tribe: Mohawk
Source: Sarah Benedict, Akwesasne Indian Land, Cornwall Island, Ontario

---

    4 wild black ducks (1 1/4 pounds each)
    or
    1 big domestic duck of approximately 5 pounds

Stuffing

    all the duck giblets
    1/3 pound of mushrooms, chopped
    8 crab apples (wild apples) or 4 green apples (core them but don't remove the skin; slice them thinly)
    1 2/3 cups of raisins or grapes, dried or fresh, cut in half
    2 cups of wild hazelnuts
    1 teaspoon of vegetable salt or coltsfoot leaves salt

Basting Sauce

    3 cups of alcoholic apple cider or 6 ounces of Calvados

a) Simmer the duck giblets for 30 minutes and remove them, but reserve 1/3 cup of cooking liquid. Cut the giblets into tiny pieces to make the stuffing. Mix them with the cooking liquid and all the other stuffing ingredients.
b) Stuff the bird cavity with the mixture and sew it up

carefully or close opening with special skewers. Prick the bird all over, to allow the fat to come out.

c) Place the duck on its back on a stand in the bottom of a dripping pan. If you have stuffing left, put it all around the bird in aluminum foil.

d) Place in the oven at 400°F for one hour. Baste the bird every 20 minutes. Reduce the heat to 350°F and roast 2 more hours, basting every 20 minutes with the cider.

Makes six servings.

If you are cooking wild ducks, one hour at 325°F will be sufficient. You must baste them every 15 minutes.
A camper can cook on an open fire if his dripping pan is covered.

WEWE
ROASTED GOOSE

Tribe: Cree
Source: Mrs. Nicholas Whiskichan, James Bay, Attawapiskat, Ontario

---

    2   white or blue geese (or Canada geese) approximately 6 pounds each
    or
    1   10 to 12 pound domestic goose

Stuffing

giblets
40 ounces of water
10 wild onions
4 cups of dried bannock (crumbled) or bread crumbs
6 stalks of celery
2 cups of red cranberries (fresh)
1/2 pound of fresh mushrooms
1 pound of dried prunes, boiled (reserve the syrup)
2 tablespoons of vegetable salt
1/2 teaspoon of black pepper
1/2 teaspoon of savory
1 medium onion or 4 wild onions
2 cups of p'tit caribou to pour over the birds while cooking

a) Simmer giblets in 1 quart of water for 30 minutes, then cut them into small pieces. Strain the cooking liquid to take off

the fat and reserve this liquid for later use.
b) For stuffing, mix the following ingredients: crushed wild onions, dried bannock, diced celery in 1/4 inch pieces, cranberries, mushrooms, prunes, syrup, salt, pepper, giblets, giblet broth, savory, onions. Fill the bird's cavity and neck area and sew up carefully.
c) Place the bird on a stand in a dripping pan and put the uncovered pan in the oven at 350°F for approximately 4 1/2 hours. Prick the skin all over, basting every 15 minutes with the p'tit caribou.

For eight very hungry white hunters.

The outdoor camper can wrap the bird in aluminum foil. If moistened thoroughly the bird will cook evenly over an open fire.

PAMAAKWE or BINE
PARTRIDGE OR GROUSE ALGONQUIN STYLE

Tribe: Ojibway
Source: Walter Axe,
Sudbury, Ontario

---

    3 grouse totalling 4 1/2 pounds
    or
    4 big partridges
    2 quarts (80 ounces) of water
    2 tablespoons of vegetable salt
  14 Jerusalem artichoke roots (or 14 new potatoes) well washed
    8 big mushrooms
  10 wild onions
  3/4 pound of cooked green beans
  1/3 teaspoon of freshly ground black pepper

a) Put the grouse and giblets in a large saucepan and add water to cover the fowl. Cover and simmer for 45 minutes.
b) Add the salt and put vegetables around the birds; add the pepper. Cover and simmer for 1 hour.
c) Slice, serve hot surrounded with the vegetables in its own broth.

Naturally you will need soup bowls to serve this dish. If you are making this recipe with partridges, you can lessen the cooking time as the partridge meat is more tender. Makes eight servings.

WABOS-WIIASS
RABBIT STEW

Tribe: Cree
Source: Bernard Assiniwi, Rivière Desert Reserve, Maniwaki, Quebec

---

 2 plump wild rabbits (diced in 1 inch pieces)
10 wild onions
 6 great burdock roots
 1 handful of fiddleheads (in the spring only)
vegetable salt to taste, thyme to taste, black pepper
20 ounces of water
 8 ounces of p'tit caribou
 8 ounces of red wine (optional)
1/2 cup of flour (wheat)
1/2 cup of butter
1/4 pound of lean pork (diced in 1 inch pieces)

a) Sauté the pork in 1 tablespoon of butter and put in a large saucepan.
b) Sauté the rabbit in the melted pork fat. Place in the saucepan.
c) Brown the wild onions in butter and pour on top of rabbits.
d) Melt half a cup of butter, add flour and thin with wine, and pour over the rabbits in saucepan.
e) Add salt, pepper, p'tit caribou, thyme and the great burdock roots, and simmer in the saucepan for 1 hour.
f) Ten minutes before serving, add fiddleheads, and serve with bannock.

Makes eight servings.

MONS-ODE-IMA
MOOSE HEART

Tribe: Cree
Source: Bernard Assiniwi, Rivière Desert Reserve, Maniwaki, Quebec

---

The heart of the moose, like that of the deer, is one of the most tender game meats.

a) You just have to brown it in melted butter in a frying pan.
b) Add a bit of thyme and pepper on top.
c) Cook in the oven at 300°F for 30 minutes. Slice it, and you will taste the greatest delicacy existing in wild game meat.

Try it when the animal is freshly killed...not three days later!

KAG
PORCUPINE

Tribe: Cree
Source: Bernard Assiniwi, Rivière Desert Reserve, Maniwaki, Quebec

---

The porcupine is very easy to kill and because of this can save the life of the lost hunter or the lost camper in the bush. It can be killed by hitting it on the nose with a small stick. Its meat can be eaten raw, without too much danger of sickness.

Some of the fat must be boiled away (for 10 minutes) if it is to be roasted in the oven or grilled over an open fire. In the oven, 300°F and 15 minutes per pound is the rule of thumb for cooking porcupine. Wild onions are good with this meat which sometimes shrinks to half its size in cooking.

The quills of this animal were used by our Indian women to decorate their garments and parkas, somewhat like embroidery. The hairs served in headdress decorations.

VEGETABLE MAIN DISHES

NADOWE-MANDAMIN
CORN, IROQUOIAN STYLE

Tribe: Mohawk
Source: John Diabo,
Brooklyn, New York

---

24 ounces of corn
3 quarts of water (120 ounces)
1/3 cup of butter or margarine
10 wild onions or shallots, finely chopped
1/4 cup of wheat flour (all purpose)
2 cups of corn flour
3 tablespoons of baking powder
2 tablespoons of maple sugar or brown sugar
1 1/2 tablespoons of coltsfoot leaves salt or sea salt
2 turtle eggs or very small hen eggs
1/2 cup of milk
1 goose carcass

a) Boil the goose carcass in about 3 quarts of water with the 10 wild onions, for 90 minutes.
b) Take out the carcass and measure 2 quarts of goose broth, in which you melt the butter, and simmer for 10 minutes.
c) Mix together corn flour, wheat flour, baking powder, sugar and salt.
d) Beat the milk and eggs together in a bowl and add this liquid to the flour mix. Then add the corn.
e) Bring the goose broth to a boil and drop in the corn mixture, one tablespoon at a time.

f) Reduce heat. When all the corn mixture has been added to the broth, stir well, cover the saucepan and simmer 15 minutes.

Serve this meal with game meat, it is very sustaining.

WANAN-BIGOSHKA
SMOKED SALMON AND EGGS

Tribe: Montagnais
Source: Mrs. Paul Ashini, Betsiamite Reserve,
Bersimis, Quebec

---

      5 wild duck eggs or 20 turtle eggs
      1/2 teaspoon of pepper
      1/4 cup of black mustard leaves (or dandelion leaves), cut into small pieces
      3 tablespoons of butter or margarine
      3/4 pound of smoked salmon, sliced in long strips

a) Beat the eggs with the pepper and add the black mustard leaves.
b) Melt the butter in a frying pan and cook the beaten eggs with the smoked salmon. Break up the eggs during cooking.

Makes five servings.

Served with roasted yellow waterlily roots, or cattail roots in hot ashes, it is delicious.

IROQUOIAN SUCCOTASH

Tribe: Tuscarora
Source: This was a national dish of the southern Iroquois, but it is also known in all the other Iroquoian tribes, such as the Oneida, Tuscarora, Cayuga, Onondaga, Mohawk, Seneca, Susquehanna, Neutral, Tobacco, Huron and Cherokee.

---

    1 pound of red kidney beans (cooked)
    20 ounces of corn
    1 pound of hamburger meat
    1/2 cup of sweet cream
    a little butter
    20 ounces of hominy
    6 wild onions or 6 shallots (minced)
    salt, pepper, wild thyme (one branch, dried)

a) In a large saucepan, brown the wild onions and the hamburger meat in butter.
b) Add the beans, corn, hominy, salt, pepper and thyme, cover and simmer on low heat for 15 minutes.
c) Uncover, add the cream, and stir, just to heat, for 10 minutes.

Serve hot. Makes six servings.

POCAHONTASI-KINAGIWIS
POCAHONTAS GARDEN

Source: *Virginia Journal*, October 1857. Probably adapted to European style, but nonetheless delicious.

    3/4 cup of white beans
    2 1/2 cups of water
    1/4 pound of salted pork or bacon (diced)
    1/2 cup of minced wild onions or 3/4 cup of minced shallots
    1/2 cup of diced carrots
    1/2 cup of diced celery
    1 cup of chopped red cabbage or 2 cups of black mustard leaves
    40 ounces of water
    2 teaspoons of vegetable salt or sea salt
    1/2 teaspoon of pepper
    1 teaspoon of maple sugar
    1/2 cup of wild rice
    16 ounces of crushed tomatoes (cooked)
    16 ounces of corn

a) Soak the beans 12 hours, then cook them in the same water for 1 hour.
b) Fry the pork to brown it. Add the vegetables and all the other ingredients except rice and tomatoes.
c) Cook for 15 minutes, well covered.
d) Add the rice and tomatoes, and cook for 15 more minutes.

Serve hot. Makes eight servings.

KINIGAWISSIN
ASSINIWI'S VEGETABLE STEW

Tribe: Cree
Source: Bernard Assiniwi, Rivière Desert Reserve, Maniwaki, Quebec

---

    1/2 pound of diced bacon
    1 diced green pepper
    3 tablespoons of butter
    1/2 diced cucumber
    10 wild onions or 10 shallots, diced
    16 ounces of cooked green peas
    16 ounces of crushed tomatoes
    1 cup of mashed Jerusalem artichoke roots or potatoes
grilled bannock, salt and pepper

a) Fry the bacon in butter with green pepper, cucumber and wild onions.
b) When tender, add peas, corn, tomatoes, Jerusalem artichokes and grilled bannock, salt and pepper.
c) Stir well, and heat until done to a turn.

It is fast and delicious.

MANDAMIN
CORN SIOUX STYLE

Tribe: Quapaw
Source: Louis Ballard, Curriculum Director, Sante-Fe School of Indian Arts, Santa-Fe, New Mexico, U.S.A.

---

    1 1/2 cups of corn
    1/4 cup of diced green pepper
    1/4 cup of diced mild red pepper
    3 tablespoons of butter
    3 wild onions or shallots with tops
    salt and pepper to taste

a) Melt the butter and fry the red and green peppers with the wild onions for 3 minutes.
b) Add the corn, salt and pepper.
c) Cook 5 to 10 minutes at low heat and serve.

MANOMIN
WILD RICE

Tribe: Ojibway
Source: Joseph Land, Kenora, Ontario
and Fort Alexander, Manitoba

---

    2 cups of wild rice (washed)
    3 cups of water
    2 1/2 teaspoons of coltsfoot leaves salt or sea salt
    10 wild onions, finely minced (or 14 shallots)
    6 big mushrooms (washed and coarsely chopped)
    4 slices of bacon
    1 cup of red kidney beans (cooked)
    1 cup corn
    1/2 cup of sweet corn
    1 egg

a) Into a large saucepan put the wild rice, water and salt and bring to a boil. Count 10 minutes. Turn off the heat, cover the saucepan and let the water be absorbed by the rice.
b) Brown the bacon, then drain it on absorbent paper. Sauté the wild onions and mushrooms in the bacon fat, and mix together bacon, wild onions and mushrooms with corn and kidney beans. Add this mixture to the wild rice.
c) Beat the egg in the cream until light, then mix well with the wild rice mixture.
d) Cover the saucepan (first grease with melted butter on the inside) and put in oven at 325°F for 30 minutes.
e) Take out of the oven, mix well and put it back uncovered for 30 minutes.

f) Take it out again, re-mix it, and put back in the oven 15 more minutes.

Makes eight servings.

N.B. The wild rice that you buy on the commercial market is very expensive but much more nourishing and delicious than brown or white rice. Once tried, it will become your favorite. If you can't afford the price asked for such a delicate food, maybe you will find the time to harvest it, when it is ripe in August. You only have to travel in a canoe for a couple of hours to harvest from 3 to 5 pounds of this natural food. Try it once...try it the Indian way...you won't regret it.

MISKODISSIMIN
BAKED BEANS, ABNAKIS STYLE

Tribe: Abnakis
Source: Théophile Panadis, Odanak Reserve, Quebec

---

    1 1/2 pounds of red kidney beans or black beans
    40 ounces of water
    3/4 pound of salted lard (fat pork) in 2 inch chunks
    or
    1   rump of beaver meat (diced)
    3/4 cup of maple syrup
    2   teaspoons of vegetable salt or sea salt
    2   teaspoons of dry mustard (the crushed seeds of black mustard are perfect)
    6   tablespoons of maple sugar
    10 wild onions or 12 shallots, coarsely chopped
    1   plump, boneless partridge
    1   cup of p'tit caribou

a) Put beans in a large saucepan and cover with water to 2 inches above the beans.
b) Add the lard or the beaver rump to the beans and simmer for 2 hours or until the beans are tender; add water if necessary.
c) Drain the beans, keeping 1 cup of cooking water.
d) In a measuring cup, mix the maple syrup, salt, dry mustard and maple sugar, then add the cooking water to make 1 1/2 cups.

e) Pour this liquid evenly over the beans; add the wild onions and p'tit caribou.
f) Put in a 3 quart earthenware pot and place in the oven at 350°F for 2 hours. The liquid should be sufficient for cooking.

This is an improved recipe dating back to the 18th century and it derives from the Penobscot and Abnakis Indian recipe for Boston baked beans.

NIND-ONSAN
WILD ONION SQUASH

Tribe: Mohawk, Oneida, Cayuga, Onondaga, Tuscarora and probably Huron, Neutral and Tobacco, too.
Source: Traditional registers of The Six-Nations Longhouse Organization, Ohsweken, Ontario

---

- 1 nice, big yellow squash
- 4 cups of fowl broth (partridge, lark, snipe, grouse or duck)
- 3 wild onions or 6 shallots with tops
- 3 tablespoons of fat from fowl
- 1/2 teaspoon of vegetable salt or sea salt
- 1/2 teaspoon of freshly ground pepper

a) Cut the squash in 4 pieces.
b) Peel it and discard the seeds.
c) Put all ingredients in a large saucepan and simmer, well covered, for 40 minutes, or until the squash is tender. Serve, sprinkling with broth.

Fried bannock is good with this meal. Serves four persons.

OSHKINIGIKWE (the Virgin)
TOMATO STEW

Tribe: Wampanoag (from Virginia)
Source: Conversation with King Philip,
Raoul Dutang, Paris 1672

---

    4 pounds of miniature Mexican tomatoes (washed and with seeds removed)
    12 wild onions or 12 shallots
    1/3 cup of water
    1/3 cup of cucumber, finely minced
    1 teaspoon of coltsfoot leaves salt or vegetable salt
    1/4 teaspoon of freshly ground pepper
    1/3 cup of corn flour

a) Place tomatoes in a large saucepan, add the wild onions and water, and simmer for 30 minutes, stirring gently and occasionally.
b) Add the cucumbers, salt and pepper and simmer for 10 minutes until the tomatoes break up when stirring.
c) Quickly add corn flour, one tablespoon at a time, stirring slowly.
d) Simmer for 5 minutes, and serve.

Makes six servings.

NIND-PINGWAWA
HOT ASHES SQUASH

Tribe: Odawa
Source: John Paul, Birch Island Reserve,
Whitefish Falls, Ontario

---

    2 yellow squash, well washed
    6 tablespoons of butter
    6 tablespoons of natural honey
    8 teaspoons of maple syrup or maple sugar
pepper and vegetable salt to taste

a) Wrap the squash in aluminum foil and place in oven at 350°F for 1 hour, or until you can prick them easily with a fork.
b) Take out of oven, peel them, cut them in half and take out the seeds.
c) Baste the two halves with butter and honey and spread 2 teaspoons of maple sugar on each half, then salt and pepper them.
d) Put back in oven at 325°F for 1 1/2 hours, basting occasionally with the juice accumulating in the squash halves.
e) Serve, basting the pieces.

Makes eight servings.

Nadowe-Mandamin
  Corn, Iroquoian Style   65
Wanan-Bigoshka
  Smoked Salmon and Eggs   67
Iroquoian Succotash   68
Pocahontasi-Kinagiwis
  Pocahontas Garden   69
Kinigawissin
  Assiniwi's Vegetable Stew   70
Mandamin
  Corn Sioux Style   71
Manomin
  Wild Rice   72
Miskodissimin
  Baked Beans, Abnakis Style   74
Nind-Onsan
  Wild Onion Squash   76
Oshkinigikwe (the Virgin)
  Tomato Stew   77
Nind-Pingwawa
  Hot Ashes Squash   78
Bodadjige-Mandamin
  Hominy Corn   80

OUTDOORSMEN

You can cook the squash in hot ashes if you pierce a hole on top first, then take out the seeds; put all the ingredients in before wrapping the squash in aluminum foil, and bury them in hot ashes. It should take approximately 2 to 3 hours to cook.

BODADJIGE-MANDAMIN
HOMINY CORN

This was the way the Iroquois preferred to eat corn. It is a simple and quickly prepared dish.

---

    32 ounces of hominy corn (two 16 ounce cans)
    4   tablespoons of butter
    4   eggs, lightly beaten
    2   teaspoons of vegetable salt
    1/8 teaspoon of freshly ground pepper

a) Drain the hominy corn, and reserve the liquid. (You need 1½ cups of liquid, if there isn't enough, add water.)
b) Heat the liquid with butter to melt.
c) Add this liquid slowly to the beaten eggs, stirring continuously; add the salt and pepper.
d) Add the hominy; mix well. Put everything in a 2 quart earthenware pot or pyrex pan. Put this pan in a dripping pan into which you have poured cold water.
e) Place in a moderate oven at 350°F and cook for 1 hour.

Serve hot. Makes six servings.

SEAFOOD AND FISH MAIN DISHES

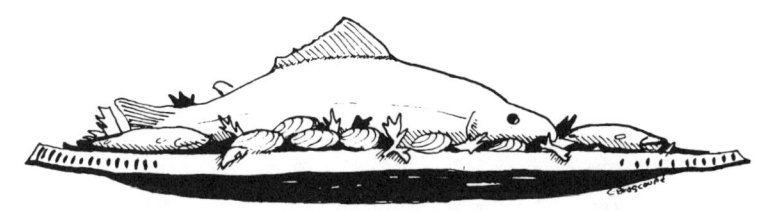

Salmon on a bed of clams.

Omakaki
  Frog Legs   83
Nibina-Midass
  Many Legs in Deep Frying Oil (Octopus)   84
Gigo-Mikwamika
  Poached Fish in Trout Jelly   85
Namegoss-Mikwamika
  Trout Jelly   86
Gigo-Pindig-Nabo
  Codfish in Mussel Sauce   87
Giwedin-Wiiass
  North West Coast Crabs   89
Gigo-Wiiass
  Grilled Salmon Steak   90
Gigo-Wiiassabo
  Poached Salmon Bella-Bella   91
Micmac-Dagonigade
  Micmac Seafood   92

OMAKAKI
FROG LEGS

Tribe: Blackfoot
Source: Alex Scalp-Lock, Blackfoot Reserve, Cluny, Alberta

---

    6 prairie chicken eggs or 3 wild duck eggs or 3 hen eggs
    1 cup of corn flour or wheat flour
    1/2 teaspoon of black pepper
    2 1/2 pounds of frog legs
    1 cup of sunflower seed oil, or corn oil or animal fat
    10 wild onions or 3 cloves of garlic

a) Mix all the dry ingredients.
b) Beat the eggs, add them to the dry ingredients and make a pancake paste.
c) Chop the wild onions finely and crush them in a mortar. Add them to the paste.
d) Dip the frog legs in the paste (be sure it is light, otherwise add water).
e) Heat the oil and drop the frog legs in it.
f) Fry them until golden and crusty.

NIBINA-MIDASS
MANY LEGS IN DEEP FRYING OIL (OCTOPUS)

Tribe: Kwakiutl
Source: Senator Guy Williams, Alert Bay Reserve, B.C.

---

    3 small octopuses (totalling 1 1/2 pounds)
    10 diced wild onions
    1 1/2 teaspoons of sea salt
    3 wild duck eggs or 10 turtle eggs or 3 hen eggs
    1 1/2 cups of sunflower seed oil or corn oil
       or melted animal fat

a) Drop the octopuses in a large saucepan of boiling water for 15 to 25 minutes. Drain and plunge into cold water.
b) With a rough brush take off the purple skin. Cut off the legs and chop them in small, rounded pieces; discard the heads.
c) Mix together the wild onions, sea salt, beaten eggs and corn flour; make a uniform mixture.
d) Dip the octopus leg pieces in this mixture.
e) Heat the oil in a frying pan and fry them with wild onions and melted butter.

It is good.

Senator Williams gave me this recipe in March 1966, while he was President of the Native Brotherhood of B.C.

GIGO-MIKWAMIKA
POACHED FISH IN TROUT JELLY

Tribe: Micmac
Source: Janet Morris, Eskasoni Reserve,
Nova Scotia

---

    1 recipe of trout jelly (see following recipe)
    6 sliced pieces of fish (halibut or salmon) 2 inches thick

a) Poach the fish pieces in trout jelly while it's cooking.
b) Place slices of fish in a deep plate or a low pyrex pan and cover with the jelly liquid.

Cool and serve.

NAMEGOSS-MIKWAMIKA
TROUT JELLY

Tribe: Micmac
Source: Janet Morris, Eskasoni Reserve,
Nova Scotia

---

    6 sea trout heads or lake trout heads
    7 cups of water
    1 1/2 teaspoons of sea salt
    1/2 cup of minced, fresh watercress
    2 tablespoons of fresh cucumber (use the gelatinous center without the seeds)
    1/4 teaspoon of freshly ground pepper

a) Boil the trout heads in water with the salt for 90 minutes.
b) Strain, adding watercress, cucumbers and pepper to the liquid.
c) Put it in a mold and cool until it becomes a firm jelly, or use it for glazing a poached fish or serve it as a side dish with fish or sea food. Oven-cooked trout or clay-cooked trout are particularly good with this jelly.

To make four cups of jelly.

GIGO-PINDIG-NABO
CODFISH IN MUSSEL SAUCE

Tribe: Micmac
Source: Wallace Labillois, Eel River Reserve, New Brunswick

---

3 dozen mussels in their shells
3/4 cup of water
4 lightly beaten eggs
1 1/4 cups of corn flour
3 teaspoons of coltsfoot leaves salt
1/2 teaspoon of freshly ground pepper
10 small cod fillets
3/4 cup plus 4 tablespoons of butter
3/4 cup of shallot tops

a) With a hard brush, clean the mussel shells and wash them in cold water.
b) Place the mussels on a stand in a big cast iron cauldron, add the water and bring to a boil.
c) Cover the cauldron, reduce heat and let the mussels steam for 20 minutes.
d) Take out the mussels from the shells and discard those shells. Chop the mussels. Keep 1/3 cup of cooking broth.
e) Put the beaten egg on a plate.
f) Put the corn flour, salt and pepper, well mixed, on a second plate.
g) Dip the cod fillets in the eggs, then in corn flour.
h) Fry the fillets in 3/4 cup of melted butter, in frying pan.

i) In a smaller frying pan, melt 4 tablespoons of butter and fry the shallot tops and the mussels. Add 1/3 cup of cooking broth. Simmer 5 minutes. Pour the sauce over the fillets and serve.

Makes ten servings.

GIWEDIN-WIIASS
NORTH WEST COAST CRABS

Tribe: Kutchin
Source: Jim Riverboat,
Dawson, Yukon

---

      1 1/2 pounds of crab meat
      4   tablespoons of melted butter
      2   wild onions, minced
      2   cups of crushed sheep sorrel (see *Survival in the Bush)*
sea salt and pepper to taste

a) Drain crab meat carefully and place in a dripping pan.
b) Cover with butter and half of the wild onions.
c) Grill for 4 minutes, season with salt and pepper, and cover with sorrel.

Serve hot. It is unbelievably good! Makes two to four servings.

GIGO-WIIASS
GRILLED SALMON STEAK

Tribe: Montagnais
Source: Chief Daniel Vachon, Seven Islands Indian Reserve, Quebec

---

    6 1 1/2 inch thick salmon steaks
    6 wild onions or 6 shallots, chopped
    sea salt and pepper
    1/4 cup of crushed sheep sorrel

a) Place wild onions on each steak to almost cover it.
b) Grill the salmon steaks on charcoal for 3 minutes on each side at about 5 to 6 inches from the flame.
c) Season with salt, pepper and sheep sorrel. If you are grilling the fish in an oven—4 to 5 minutes will be necessary for each side.

Makes six servings.

GIGO-WIIASSABO
POACHED SALMON BELLA-BELLA

Tribe: Bella-Bella
Source: Barbara Wilson, Haida Indian from Queen Charlotte Islands, British Columbia

---

    6 1 1/2 inch thick salmon steaks
  12 big mushrooms, sliced
    2 teaspoons chopped watercress
    4 wild onions or 6 shallots with tops
  40 ounces of fowl broth (partridge, hen, etc.)
    3 teaspoons of vegetable salt
  1/2 teaspoon of black pepper, freshly ground
    2 cups of crushed sheep sorrel, for the juice only

a) Simmer mushrooms, watercress and wild onions in broth for 10 minutes. Season with salt and pepper.
b) Cool to room temperature, refrigerate until ready to poach the salmon.
c) Place the salmon in frying pan and cover with the liquid.
d) Simmer 15 to 20 minutes.

Baste with cooking juice and sprinkle with sheep sorrel juice and serve. Makes six servings.

MICMAC-DAGONIGADE
MICMAC SEAFOOD

Tribe: Micmac
Source: Wallace Labillois, Eel River Reserve, New Brunswick

- 3 dozen oysters in shells
- 3 dozen periwinkles
- 3 dozen mussels in shells
- 3 dozen clams in shells
- 8 ears of corn in the yellow husk
- 8 Jerusalem artichoke roots, unpeeled
- 8 small lobsters of about 1 1/4 pounds each (green, live lobsters)
- 3 quarts of salted water (with 3 tablespoonsful of sea salt)
- 12 ounces of white wine or dandelion wine

a) Clean oysters, mussels and clams with a hard brush, and rinse with cold water.
b) Carefully husk the corn, removing the outer green leaves and leaving the yellow husk on.
c) Clean the Jerusalem artichokes with a hard brush.
d) In a large cast iron pot with a tightly-fitting lid, place alternately the oysters in the bottom, 4 lobsters, 4 ears of corn, 8 Jerusalem artichokes, and finish with the 4 remaining lobsters and 4 ears of corn. Cover with the periwinkles, mussels and clams.
e) Pour salt water over the seafood, cover tightly and seal with dough around the cover.

f) Bring to a boil and boil for 3 minutes.
g) Lower the heat and simmer 2 hours. Serve.

Makes eight servings.

If you are vacationing on the seashore, you can replace the salted water using half sea water and half fresh water.

DESSERTS

Nuts, strawberries, cherries, apples – Indian desserts.

Indian desserts are simple and delicious. Almost always they consist of wild fruits and natural foods.

Pagan-Wiiagiminan	
Maple Nuts	97
Sisibakwat-Okwemin	
Sugared Cherries	98
Mashkigimin-Onagan	
Traditional Cranberry Sauce	99
Jabomin	
Wild Red Currents	100
Mashkigimin-Dagonigade	
Stewed Cranberries	102
Mishimini-Okonass	
Wild Apple Sauce	103
Mishimin	
Apples on Charcoal	104
Anish-Nah-Be Mandamin	
Indian Delight	105
Ogwissiman	
Honeyed Pumpkin	106
Miskwimin Amo Sisibakwat	
Honeyed Raspberries	107
Winnissimin	
Blueberry Bannock	108

PAGAN-WIIAGIMINAN
MAPLE NUTS

Tribe: Algonquin (Quebec)
Source: *The Diary of Sister Marie de la Nouvelle France,* leaflet held at Musée de l'Homme, Paris (1739)

---

    8 ounces of grated maple sugar
    6 ounces of water
    4 ounces of broken wild hazelnuts
    3 ounces of walnuts or acorns
  14 ounces of wild dried prunes (stoned)

a) Place maple sugar and water in large saucepan. Heat slowly without stirring.
b) Take off the heat, drop the walnuts in this hot syrup and stir to be sure all parts will be sugared. Then drop alternately, hazelnuts and prunes, and stir well.
c) Take everything out with a skimming ladle and cool. If there is any syrup left, eat it with bannock.

The sugared nuts are simply delectable. Makes seven servings.

SISIBAKWAT-OKWEMIN
SUGARED CHERRIES

Tribe: Okanagan
Source: Mrs. Godfriedson,
Okanagan Falls, B.C.

---

    2 1/2 pounds of giant B.C. cherries
    1 1/2 cups of maple sugar
    1 cup of water or preferably p'tit caribou

a) Put maple sugar and water or p'tit caribou in a saucepan and boil for 15 minutes.
b) Add cherries and simmer 10 minutes.
c) Turn off heat, cool and eat fresh with bannock.

Makes five servings.

MASHKIGIMIN-ONAGAN
TRADITIONAL CRANBERRY SAUCE

Tribe: Algonquin
Source: Mary Commanda, Rivière Desert Reserve,
Maniwaki, Quebec

---

      1 1/2 pounds of wild, high bush cranberries or domestic cranberries
      2 cups of maple sugar
      1 1/2 cups of birch sap or spring water

a) Place all ingredients in a large saucepan and bring to a boil. Reduce heat and simmer 25 to 30 minutes.
b) Cool and serve with wild meat such as bear, beaver or spruce grouse.

It is also very good spread on bannock bread.

JABOMIN
WILD RED CURRENTS

Tribe: Algonquin
Source: Mary Commanda, Rivière Desert Reserve, Maniwaki, Quebec

---

  2 1/2 cups of all purpose wheat flour
  3/4 cup of corn flour, plus 3 tablespoons
  3/4 teaspoon of baking powder
  1 1/2 teaspoons of vegetable salt
  1 cup of butter
  1 1/4 cups of boiling water
  2 pounds of fresh currents (crushed and sugared) in syrup
  2 tablespoons of honey
  1 cup of pulverized sheep sorrel (to make a juice)

a) Mix together 3/4 cup of corn flour, baking powder and salt.
b) Using two knives, cut the butter into this mix.
c) Pour boiling water over and mix fast.
d) Divide this dough in half, spread one half in the bottom and sides of a pyrex pan which you have already buttered.
e) Spread 1 1/2 tablespoons of corn flour over it.
f) Crush half of the currents in their syrup and add the rest of the currents whole. Add the honey and sheep sorrel juice or crushed sheep sorrel (if there is no juice), then put in the pyrex pan.
g) Cover with remaining dough and spread 1 1/2 tablespoons of corn flour on top.

h) Place in oven at 400°F for 35 to 40 minutes to brown the top. Cut and serve.

You can make the same dish using raspberries, blueberries or strawberries. Makes five servings.

MASHKIGIMIN-DAGONIGADE
STEWED CRANBERRIES

Tribe: Algonquin
Source: Noé Kistabish, Dominion Reserve Abitibi, Quebec

    1/3 cup of butter
    3/4 cup of maple sugar
    1 1/2 cups of pure honey
    3   beaten eggs
    2   cups of fresh wild cranberries (high bush or low bush)
    3   cups of flour
    1   teaspoon of vegetable salt

a) Make a cream mixing the honey, butter and maple sugar.
b) Add beaten eggs and crushed cranberries to the buttered cream.
c) Mix together flour and salt and add to first mix little by little.
d) Place in a well-buttered and floured low, earthenware pan. Close cover tightly with dough.
e) Make a hole in the ashes of an open fire and cover with hot ashes.
f) Cook for 3 to 4 hours, take out, cool and serve.

MISHIMINI-OKONASS
WILD APPLE SAUCE

Tribe: Mohawk
Source: Jean-Paul Simon, Lake of Two Mountains, Oka, Quebec

---

    4 pounds of wild crab apples (core them but do not peel), cut in slices
    8 ounces of maple sugar (1/2 pound)
    4 cups of water

a) Place all ingredients together in large saucepan.
b) Bring to a boil and reduce heat.
c) Simmer 50 minutes, stirring frequently.

Serve hot on bannock.

MISHIMIN
APPLES ON CHARCOAL

Tribe: Mohawk
Source: Jean-Paul Simon, Lake of Two Mountains, Oka, Quebec

---

    6 nice, big apples
    1/4 pound of maple sugar

a) Core apples with a sharp knife.
b) Fill cavity with maple sugar.
c) Wrap in aluminum foil.
d) Roast 10 minutes on charcoal broiler.
e) Turn to other side and repeat.
f) So as not to lose the sugared liquid, twirl foil closed around apple.

ANISH-NAH-BE MANDAMIN
INDIAN DELIGHT

Tribe: Mohawk
Source: Jean-Paul Simon, Lake of Two Mountains, Oka, Quebec

---

    3 cups of all purpose flour
    1 3/4 cups of corn flour
    1 teaspoon baking soda
    2 teaspoons vegetable salt
    3 1/2 cups of milk
    2 cups of maple syrup
    3/4 cup of fresh corn

a) Mix together all the dry ingredients.
b) Mix together maple syrup and milk.
c) Add dry ingredients to liquid ones.
d) Pour into a well-buttered earthenware pan and cover.
e) Put this pan on a stand inside a deep cauldron that can be closed tightly.
f) Pour boiling water in the cauldron to reach half-way up the earthenware pan. Cover well and let cook for at least 3 hours.
g) Take the earthenware pan out and let rest for 40 minutes; uncover it and let rest 20 more minutes.
h) Using a spatula, unmould this Indian delight, and turn it up-side down.

Served hot or cold, it is equally good. Makes twelve servings.

OGWISSIMAN
HONEYED PUMPKIN

Tribe: Mohawk and Algonquin
Source: Jean-Paul Simon, Lake of Two Mountains, Oka, Quebec and
Mary Commanda, Rivière Desert Reserve, Maniwaki, Quebec

---

    1 small pumpkin
    1/4 cup of honey
    1/4 cup of apple cider
    1/4 cup of butter or margarine

a) Wash the pumpkin, wrap it in aluminum foil and place in the oven at 325°F for 1 1/2 hours.
b) Take out of oven, pierce a 4 inch hole on top of pumpkin, take out the seeds and loose pulp.
c) Mix together honey, cider and melted butter; brush the inside walls of the pumpkin with this mixture.
d) Place pumpkin cover on the hole and put back in oven for 35 to 40 minutes, basting occasionally.
e) Cut pieces for your guests and baste these pieces while serving. You can also cook this pumpkin in open fire ashes, but you will have to wrap it in soaked newspaper over aluminum foil, or use special charcoal wrappings.

Makes eight servings.

MISKWIMIN AMO SISIBAKWAT
HONEYED RASPBERRIES

Source: All Tribes

---

1 quart of well-washed raspberries
2 cups of pure honey

Crush the raspberries in the honey and serve.

WINNISSIMIN
BLUEBERRY BANNOCK

Tribe: Odawa
Source: Rose-Marie Pelletier Fisher,
Wikwimikong Indian Reserve, Manitoulin Island, Ontario

- 24 ounces of fresh blueberries
- 5 cups of all purpose flour
- 1 cup of maple sugar
- 4 teaspoons of baking powder
- 3 1/2 cups of shortening or corn oil or sunflower seed oil
- 6 eggs

a) Press the blueberries to obtain approximately 1/2 cup of juice.
b) Mix together all the dry ingredients.
c) Pour vegetable oil in a deep frying pan and heat.
d) Beat the eggs with the blueberry juice to get a deep cream.
e) Mix cream with dry ingredients and add blueberries.
f) Drop this dough in hot oil, one tablespoon at a time, and brown it until it's a chocolate color.
g) Serve hot with mint tea.

Makes four dozen biscuits.

BEVERAGES

Kijiga
  Maple Drink 111
Amo-Sisibakwat
  Honey Drink 112
Mashkossiw-Nabo
  Dandelion Wine, the "Old Way" 113
Ashkote-Nibish
  "P'tit Caribou" 115

KIJIGA
MAPLE DRINK

Tribe: Cree
Source: Bernard Assiniwi, Rivière Desert, Maniwaki, Quebec

---

    1 cup of maple sugar
    10 cups of water (80 ounces)

a) Put ingredients in a deep saucepan and simmer 20 to 25 minutes, stirring gently.
b) Serve hot or ice cold.

For the gourmets, cognac is excellent in this drink.
For the Indians, p'tit caribou is delectable and heady.

AMO-SISIBAKWAT
HONEY DRINK

Tribe: Cree
Source: Bernard Assiniwi, Rivière Desert, Maniwaki, Quebec

---

      40 ounces of water
      10 ounces of honey

Heat water slightly and add honey. Simmer 10 minutes, cool and serve ice cold.

It is good with rum or with "p'tit caribou", to taste.

MASHKOSSIW-NABO
DANDELION WINE, THE "OLD WAY"

Tribe: Several Eastern Tribes
Source: Many old men have passed this recipe on with a light smile on their faces.

Historians tell us that the Indians knew nothing of alcoholic beverages until the Europeans came to our continent. Our wise old men tell us this is not true and that old traditional recipes passed on from generations gone by are made by the women in the spring of each year. One of these recipes is for a kind of "dandelion wine" or brew. Another is for corn beer made by American Indians in the South.

In the spring, women harvested young dandelion leaves and gathered in the center of the village to chew the leaves. They spit them back into a large birch-bark basket, which was waterproofed with spruce gum. Human saliva being the best fermentation element, this wine, after being strained at the end of the 50th or 60th day, had sometimes become approximately 3 or 4 percent alcohol.

Corn beer was made mainly by Iroquois from the South, such as the Tuscaroras and Susquehannas, and was always kept for the annual celebration of the corn festival.

This way of making low proof alcoholic beverages might seem to be disgusting to people today, but try to remember how wine was made on the Continent during the same period! And try to keep in mind that the saliva was transformed in the fermentation process so that it lost any capacity to spread sickness in the alcohol. But in Europe dirty feet were washed in grape juice.

These wines made by the Indians were not comparable to the 90 percent alcoholic beverages imported by the settlers and which were sometimes mixed with lye or javel water, and then diluted with water.

ASHKOTE-NIBISH
"P'TIT CARIBOU"

Tribes: Micmac, Malecite, Abnakis, Montagnais, Nascopis, Algonquin, Tête de Boule, Cree, Odawa (Ottawa), Ojibway, Potawatomi, Chippewa, Huron, Mohawk, Seneca, Tuscarora, Oneida

---

    40 ounces of white alcohol, 30 percent
    40 ounces of sherry or Canadian port
      or Branvin

Mix both ingredients in a large bowl or in an earthenware jug and cool it. We used to bury it in the ground. This is a delicious and mild-tasting beverage, but take care—it produces the effect desired by the traders who showed us how to make it. They used to make us drink until drunk so they could get our furs for nothing.

As we like it.

FOR THE OUTDOORSMAN

The best way to build an "open oven." This heat reflecting wall will also warm the camper in front of his temporary shelter.

Notes for the Outdoorsman 120
Pemmigan
  Indian Style Hamburger 123
Gaskide-Wiiass
  Dried Meat 125
Namegoss
  Trout in Clay 127
Maja-Megoss
  B.B.Q. Salmon, Kwakiutl Style 129
Wiiass
  Fresh Game Meat Cooked over an Open Fire 131
Gigo
  Grilled Walleye (Doré) 133
Nind Abwe Kitchi Wiiass
  Big Game Meat (Trader Dish) 134
Kitchi Wiiass
  Game Meat on Embers 136
Kanifon-Ya-Wiiass
  Game Steak, California Indian Style 138
Pagwadj-Aiiaa
  Game Steak, Algonkian Style 140
Anish-Nah-Be Mons-Oshtigwanima
  Moose Head, Algonkian Style 142
Makwassiniwi
  Cubed Bear, Assiniwi Style 144
Alisemole-Wiiass
  Beer Mutton Chops, Seminole Style from Florida 145
Paganan-Bine
  Butternut Partridge 146
Spruce Grouse or Rock Cornish Game Hen or Pigeon 147

Trout on the Grill	149
Newspaper Trout	150
Seafood Brochettes on Cedar Sticks	151
Shrimps on Cedar Sticks	153
Grilled Lobster	155
Seafood over an Open Fire	157
Potatoes, Corn, Beaver Tail	159
Huron Sagamite, Assiniwi Style	160
Huron Sagamite	161

NOTES FOR THE OUTDOORSMAN

COOKING
For cooking game or domestic meat, one must know not to cook it directly over the flame of a fire but over the embers or in the "blue flame," otherwise the meat will be tough. To know how to build an open fire oven, see the illustration on page 117.

THE GRILL
For the "charcoal broiler" cooks, it is good to know that the charcoal should burn for approximately 30 minutes, or until it turns grey, before meat is placed over it.

AROMA
In Indian cooking, wood chips were used to give a special aroma to smoked meats. You must soak the wood chips in water for 12 hours and while the meat is cooking or smoking, you throw wet chips on the fire and the smoke takes on the aroma of whatever kind of wood you use. Recommended wood for chips: hickory, maple, ash, walnut.

GINGER ROOT
Ginger root was first imported to Canada around 1754. Since then it has been used in many Indian dishes. Fresh roots have a better taste than the ground powder. Before the advent of ginger root, we used the pepper root. This is a broadleafed plant found in swamps. We dried the root and used it as a medicine and spice.

SOYA SAUCE
In special recipes, I recommend soya sauce, a relatively recent import for us, but it is a good substitute for another import dating back even further — molasses, which we salted before using. Soya sauce tastes like salted molasses.

GAMY MEAT

Aging meat by hanging it to give it a spicier taste is not recommended to the novice. Instead, we recommend pickling the meat for 24 hours before cooking it. This is a much more reassuring method as gamy meat could be poisonous if you don't know when to stop it.

Soak a piece of meat for 24 hours in the following mixture:

2/3 cup of corn oil
1/2 cup of soya sauce
1/3 cup of "p'tit caribou"
6 wild onions or 10 shallots, well minced
3 tablespoons of grated ginger root
2 teaspoons of freshly ground pepper
1 teaspoon of dry mustard (wild black mustard seeds are good)
1/3 cup of wine vinegar to 1/2 cup of minced wood sorrel

When you are pickling meat, it is important to keep the blood of the killed animal. It is particularly good used in sauces. Blood has a high nutritional value when fresh. Four tablespoons of blood are equivalent in vitamins and minerals to 5 pounds of well-cooked meat or 10 eggs.

SEASONINGS

Several spices suggested in this book are imported from Europe, but we believe that 400 years of use allow us to say they are now part of our culture.

MILK AND CREAM

Shortly after the arrival of cows in our land, Iroquoians and Algonkians learned to like milk and cream. But one must not believe that we weren't familiar with these ingredients before that time, and that we did not know how to milk an animal! The Crees and Montagnais sometimes used moose milk to save a recently born baby who had lost his mother.

How to grind dried meat between two stones, if it has been cut against the grain — use short strokes.

PEMMIGAN
INDIAN STYLE HAMBURGER

Tribes: All Prairie Tribes
Source: Joe Saddleback, Cree, Hobbema Indian Reserve, Alberta

---

    1 pound of ground dried meat
    or
    1 pound of beef hamburger meat
    2 cups of animal fat or shortening
    2 duck eggs or hen eggs
    some maple sugar

a) Break the eggs on the meat and work it like dough.
b) Mix in the animal fat or shortening.
c) Add maple sugar and mix well.
d) Make small balls and serve.

Instead of maple sugar, fresh, wild berries were often used. This pemmican was made by the ton in the last century so that the Indian communities could spend the winter, comfortably well fed. During the 1870s and until the '90s, the American cavalry frequently destroyed these food provisions in order to force the Indians to give away their land.

Slice the meat thinly and hang the pieces on the rungs of the tripod. When one side is dry, turn the pieces over. Drying meat this way takes from two to six hours.

GASKIDE-WIIASS
DRIED MEAT

Tribe: All Tribes of America

---

      moose or deer meat
      beef or sheep, thin slices—3/4 to 1 1/4 inches, not more

Make a fire. Place a tripod over it and attach branches as shown in the illustration.
Hang the meat and let it dry, turn and do the same.
This meat can be preserved even through hot summer days.

If all non-Indian hunters would only smoke the outside crust of the game flesh or dry the top layer of flesh when hunting in hot weather, they would lose less meat.

You should try it before judging!

a) Hold the trout by the neck with left hand.
b) Press the abdomen between thumb and index finger from the head to the excretory canal to get rid of inedible matter.

NAMEGOSS
TROUT IN CLAY

Tribe: Cree and Algonquin
Source: My Father, Leonidas . . .

---

      a big salmon or rainbow trout
      thyme
      clay

a) Do not take the silt off the trout.
b) Clean the inedible material out of the fish, using the facing illustration as a guide.
c) Spread thyme around the trout.
d) Wrap the trout in an envelope of fresh clay mud, 1/2 inch thick. Bury it in hot ashes for 2 hours.
e) Break the clay on one side, and eat, using the intact piece of clay as a plate.
f) The liver and heart make a delicious sauce.

You can also cook the trout in an oven at 350°F for about 3 hours, but the taste is different.

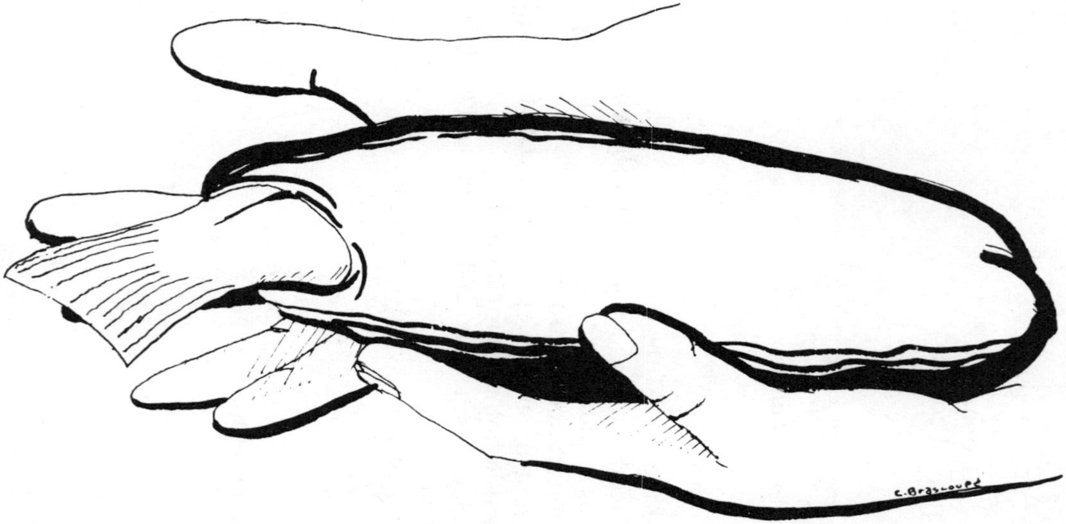

Enclose the fish in the clay and put it in the fire embers. Be sure the fish is completely covered with clay, otherwise it will dry out.

MAJA-MEGOSS
B.B.Q. SALMON, KWAKIUTL STYLE

Tribe: Kwakiutl-Shuswap
Source: Chief Simon Baker, Cappilano Reserve,
North Vancouver, B.C.

Take a nice, big salmon and clean it. Open it and spread out the two parts. Place on a grill made out of ash-wood, and attach with small pieces of wood as shown in the illustration on the introductory page 117 of this chapter, over an open fire oven. Place on reflection wall as shown, facing the south. Light a fire in front and cook for 10 to 15 minutes.

From coast to coast, this reflecting wall is built the same way by Indians.

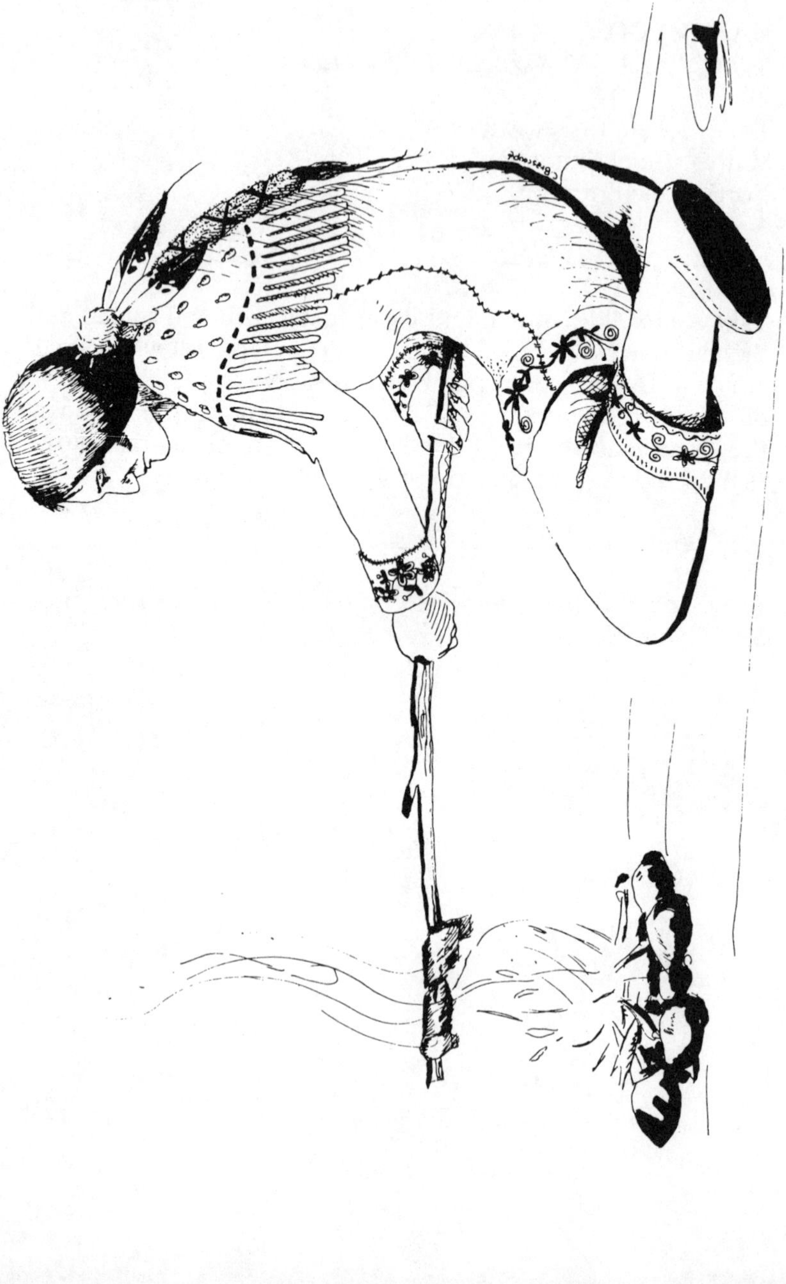

WIIASS
FRESH GAME MEAT COOKED OVER AN OPEN FIRE

Tribes: Common to All Indian Groups in Canada and U.S.A.

---

a) Cut pieces of fresh game meat, approximately 2 inches thick and 4 to 5 inches in diameter.
b) Make a fire with cedar wood.
c) Place meat on wooden forks and grill it. Salt after cooking, not before.

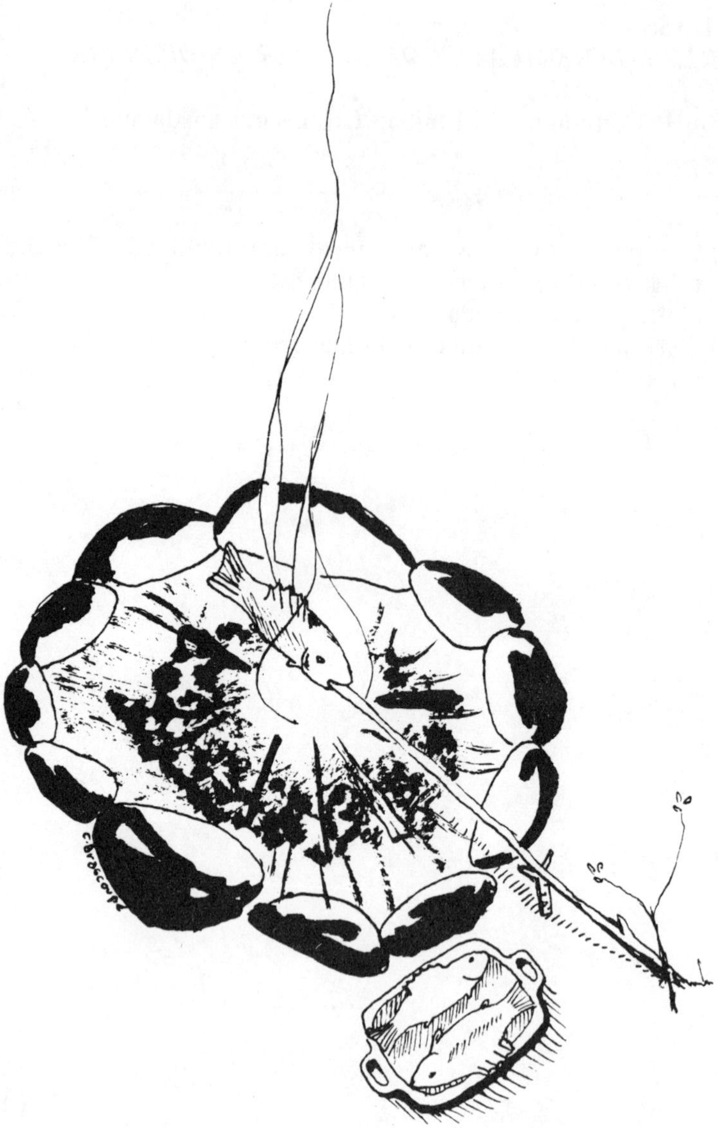

GIGO
GRILLED WALLEYE (DORE)

---

    1 nice walleye
    salt, pepper to taste

a) Scrape well to remove the scales.
b) Clean it, keeping the head well fixed to the body.
c) Take a 6-foot pole and fix the big, sharp end in the ground at a 45° angle so the small end is just over the fire.
d) Fix the fish at this small end, by opening the mouth, and inserting the pole in it. Grill it until tender.

If you are equipped to sew up the fish abdomen, you can stuff it with wild hazelnuts. This is also very good.

NIND ABWE KITCHI WIIASS
BIG GAME MEAT (TRADER DISH)

---

    piece of moose, deer or caribou
    6   pounds of shoulder rolled roast or rump roast

Marinade
    1/2 cup of corn or sunflower seed oil
    1/2 cup of p'tit caribou
    8   wild onions or 2 small, domestic onions (minced)
    3   cloves of garlic (crushed)
    2   tablespoons of freshly ground ginger root
    1   teaspoon of dry mustard
    1/3 cup of cider vinegar (or wine vinegar)
    1/2 cup of soya sauce or molasses salted with sea salt

a) Mix all marinade ingredients together.
b) Place the roast in a large bowl and pour the marinade over it.
c) Leave meat in this solution and turn every half hour.
d) Take 2 or 3 handfuls of wooden hickory chips and soak them in the water for 30 minutes.
e) Place charcoal at the rear of the broiler and light it.
f) At the front of the broiler, place aluminum foil to catch drippings from the roast.
g) Spread wood chips over charcoal to produce smoke, and place roast at the front above aluminum foil.

h) Cover the rear part of broiler.
i) Turn the roast frequently to cook well. The smoke will give it a hickory taste.

Makes eight servings.

One to one and a half hours will be necessary to cook the meat according to your taste; one hour for rare; one and a half hours for medium rare.

KITCHI WIIASS
GAME MEAT ON EMBERS

This can be done on wood fire embers, but we advise the uninitiated to do it using a broiler and charcoal.

    4 pounds of game meat
    4 wild onions or 2 cloves of garlic
    1 cup of vegetable salt or iodized salt
    4 tablespoons of freshly ground pepper
    1 tablespoon of ground ginger root
   watercress to garnish

a) Take meat out of refrigerator to allow it to come to room temperature. Insert garlic and wild onions in the roast. Mix together salt, pepper and ginger. Rub well all parts of roast with this dry mixture to form a hard crust.
b) Spread 2 inches of wood charcoal all over grill, light and wait until a white ash forms evenly. With a soaked newspaper, remove the white ash and place the roast directly on the charcoal (not on a stand) for at least 10 minutes. Turn the roast until completely cooked. The meat will be crusty on top, but rare and tender inside.
c) Ten minutes before serving, you can drop 2 or 3 wild onions on charcoal, to give a better aroma.
d) Place on a maple wood plate, and garnish with fresh water-

cress. Cut in diagonal strips approximately 1/8 inch thick and serve with baked tomatoes or baked Jerusalem artichokes.

Makes four servings.

KANIFON-YA-WIIASS
GAME STEAK, CALIFORNIA INDIAN STYLE

Allow 1 pound of meat for each guest, preferably a sirloin cut, but other cuts may be acceptable.

    1/2 to 2/3 cup of melted butter
    2 teaspoons of garlic salt

a) Mix together garlic salt and butter and rub your steaks with this mixture, then put all aside while you prepare the basting solution.

BASTING SOLUTION
    8 ounces of orange juice
    6 ounces of tomato juice
    4 to 6 ounces of minced black olives (Spanish)
    1 ounce of dried raisins
    1 tablespoon of soya sauce
    1 tablespoon of minced wild onions
    1 teaspoon of garlic salt
    1 teaspoon of fresh garlic (crushed)
    1/4 teaspoon of red cayenne pepper

b) In a large saucepan, mix all ingredients, except fresh garlic, and simmer 20 to 25 minutes, stirring constantly.
c) Add fresh garlic and simmer 20 more minutes.

d) Light the grill and let the flame die before cooking steaks.
e) Grill steaks, basting frequently.

Excellent with wild rice and potatoes.

PAGWADJ-AIIAA
GAME STEAK, ALGONKIAN STYLE

---

one piece of meat fillet 2 1/2 to 3 pounds
3   tablespoons of butter
4   minced wild onions or 6 shallots
12 big mushrooms (sliced)
1/2 cup of p'tit caribou or 1/2 cup of cognac
1/2 teaspoon of thyme

a) Sauté the wild onions in butter, then add mushrooms and p'tit caribou or cognac and thyme; simmer to thicken.
b) Make a cut all along the piece of meat and stuff this cut with the mixture.
c) Tie the meat with a butcher string in 4 places.
d) Place on grill on a deep tin plate.
e) Cook on charcoal for 40 to 50 minutes.
f) Baste occasionally with p'tit caribou and butter.

Makes four servings.

ANISH-NAH-BE MONS-OSHTIGWANIMA
MOOSE HEAD, ALGONKIAN STYLE

A deer or a caribou head can also be cooked this way. But I do not recommend the beef cattle head, unless you are sure it is from a freshly killed animal.

a) You need a freshly killed moose head with the skin and hair on. You must remove the eyes carefully, so as not to damage the brain.
b) Make a hole in the ground, approximately 3 feet deep and 3 feet wide.
c) Place stones in the bottom and on the walls of the pit, and make a fire of hardwood in it (oak wood is recommended, but maple, elm and even the yellow birch can make a good fire). Throw a couple of stones in this fire.
d) While the wood is burning, wrap the moose head in a special B.B.Q. burlap, or 3 layers of ordinary burlap, well-soaked in water, and tie with a good wire that has a long loop on the top so you can pull it out of the fire ashes when cooked.
e) When your fire is reduced to embers, push some away to place the moose head in it, cover it all with the embers, taking care to leave the "loop handle" sticking out of the fire.
f) Cover this ember fire with soaked burlap or a thick layer of wet newspapers, to retain some humidity in the heat.

How to cook moose head or deer head in hot ashes. How to make the fire and how to arrange the stones.

g) Seal the burlap edges all around the fire with earth to keep the head inside.
h) Cook all night, or at least 8 to 12 hours, depending on size of animal.
i) When cooked, remove the head from the ember fire by pulling on the loop handle. Take off the skin (when cooked, the skin is easy to remove). Slice meat around the head, and place on a plate, decorated with fresh watercress, for the first plate. A 900-pound moose can give you from 6 to 15 pounds of meat around the head.
j) Take the tongue out, slice it, and place on a second plate decorated with thyme and parsley or watercress.
k) Take the brain out of its cavity, make thin slices and place on a third plate, sprinkled with well-crushed sheep sorrel or lemon juice. Watercress is the nicest decoration for these gourmet delicacies.
l) Melted butter with garlic is an excellent sauce for these hors-d'oeuvres. Wild onions, crushed and mixed with butter are also delicious. Bannock bread is good on the side. Cold or raw potatoes are also excellent, when dipped in wild onions and melted butter.

Raw carrots, cucumbers, celery and tomatoes are also good companions to moose head meat.

MAKWASSINIWI
CUBED BEAR, ASSINIWI STYLE

---

3 pounds of bear rump meat, cut in 1 1/2 inch cubes
3/4 teaspoon of vegetable salt
3/4 teaspoon of freshly ground pepper
1 teaspoon of thyme
1 cup of minced wild onions
1 tablespoon of maple sugar or brown sugar
1/4 cup of soya sauce (or soya molasses) to replace salted molasses
1 teaspoon of freshly ground ginger root
1/4 cup of lemon juice, or 2 cups of crushed sheep sorrel

a) Place the bear meat cubes in a skillet, frying pan or in a shallow bowl (to pickle the meat).
b) Mix all other ingredients well and pour over the meat; let pickle for 6 hours.
c) Drain, and keep this pickling juice. Place bear meat cubes on grill 1/4 inch apart, but at least 3 inches away from the charcoal. Grill for approximately 5 minutes, then baste cubes all around frequently with pickling juice, until meat is well cooked and crusty. This should take approximately 25 minutes.

NOTE: Maple wood chips, soaked in water for 30 minutes and thrown on the charcoal, produce a pleasant, smoky taste in bear meat. Makes six servings.

ALISEMOLE-WIIASS
BEER MUTTON CHOPS, SEMINOLE STYLE FROM FLORIDA

Tribe: Seminole-Florida
Source: Roger Onçeola, from Florida, as told by this Indian medicine man, at Maniwaki Pow-Wow in September 1969

---

    8   mutton chops (bear, deer or caribou are also good this way)
    1/3 pound butter
    2 or 3 nice oranges
    1   cup corn meal (corn flour) or all purpose wheat flour
    1 1/2 teaspoons sea salt
    1/2 teaspoon of freshly ground pepper
    1/2 cup of beer

a) Light your fire and wait until charcoal is covered with ashes.
b) Holding a large saucepan at approximately 2 inches from the fire, melt butter.
c) In a 1 1/2-quart bowl, press the oranges and discard pulp and peel.
d) Add flour, seasonings, beer and mix well.
e) Dip the chops in this mix.
f) Place on grill for 15 minutes, each side.
g) Serve with pieces of orange.

PAGANAN-BINE
BUTTERNUT PARTRIDGE

6 partridge breasts (or chicken breasts)
1/4 pound of butter
1/4 cup of wild hazelnuts
1/4 cup of wild watercress
4 chopped wild onions
1 teaspoon dried thyme
whipping cream (35%) for brushing
sea salt and fresh pepper

a) Melt butter, mix together all other ingredients, except the cream, and put it in the blender to make a paste. Mix all with the butter, then place in refrigerator to cool; if you have no blender, crush these hazelnuts with a bottle.
b) Make a long cut into each partridge breast, and put in some of this mixture. Close cuts with tooth-picks.
c) Cook bone side of breasts on grill, then the flesh side at 4 to 5 inches from the charcoal. Brush some cream on breasts, as soon as they start to turn golden. Before eating, season with salt and pepper to taste.

SPRUCE GROUSE OR ROCK CORNISH GAME HEN OR PIGEON

Not so long ago we used to have millions of turtle-doves passing by our territory each spring, and staying with us all summer. These doves were passenger pigeons and they flew in great flocks. They were used to make pies with cornmeal crusts. French Canadians quickly adopted this meal which they called "tourtière" and made it their national dish. The birds were hunted so extensively that they disappeared forever, by the grace of civilization.

    12 wild onions or 12 shallots
    2   cloves of garlic, minced
    1/4 cup of butter
    12 big mushrooms, thinly sliced
    1/2 teaspoon of sea salt
    1   pinch of black pepper
    6   tablespoons of corn oil or sunflower seed oil
    1   teaspoon of thyme
    6   teaspoons of butter
    6   big pigeons, or rock cornish game hens, or spruce grouse
    aluminum foil

a) Cook wild onions and garlic in butter, but do not brown.

b) Mix the wild onions, garlic, mushrooms, salt, pepper, 2 teaspoons of oil and 3/4 teaspoon of thyme well.
c) Put 1 teaspoon of butter in each bird cavity. Divide stuffing mixture in 6 parts and stuff all birds. Close openings with tooth-picks or skewers.
d) Brush with oil and remaining thyme.
e) Cut 6 pieces of aluminum foil and wrap the birds individually. Cook the birds, not directly over fire, but a bit apart, for approximately 1 1/2 hours, turning every 15 minutes. Serve directly on foil paper to keep the juicy sauce.

TROUT ON THE GRILL

    6 medium trout
sea salt to taste
1/3 cup of Canadian sherry
1/3 cup of melted butter
2 tablespoons of lemon juice
6 strips of bacon

Sauce

2 teaspoons of crushed wild acorns
1/4 cup of butter
1 tablespoon of Canadian sherry
1 tablespoon of lemon juice

a) Salt inside each trout.
b) Mix sherry, butter and lemon juice, pour over trout, and pickle for 1 hour, turning after 30 minutes.
c) Drain pickle juice and wrap bacon around trout.
d) Cook on red charcoal until bacon is crusty, basting with pickling juice, turn only once.
Sauce: While cooking, brown acorns in butter, then add sherry and lemon juice. Serve hot, basting trout first.

NEWSPAPER TROUT

    1   14 inch trout
    4   tablespoons of clam juice
    2   tablespoons of minced clams (cooked)
    2   tablespoons of minced mushrooms
melted butter
    1   strip of crisp bacon, cut in small pieces
vinegar dipped watercress
    1   complete tabloid-type newspaper. Select a thick publication on a day with a lot of advertising.

a) Make a charcoal fire and let the flame die.
b) Do not remove head or tail from the trout.
c) Brush clam juice inside and out.
d) Mix mushrooms and remaining clam juice together.
e) Soak the newspaper (it has to be soaked for 15 minutes) and oil its inside with corn oil.
f) Place trout on oily side of newspaper, spread mushrooms around the trout, spread melted butter over it.
g) Roll paper around the trout and seal ends with a soaked string.
h) Cook on grill, approximately 3 minutes on each side, twice. Serve on a plate, garnished with vinegar dipped watercress, surrounded with bacon pieces.

Makes one serving.

SEAFOOD BROCHETTES ON CEDAR STICKS

---

12 scallops
12 green shrimps
12 pieces of lobster meat (size of scallops)
12 miniature Mexican tomatoes
12 mushrooms
12 pieces of fresh green pepper or 12 wild onions or 12 shallots
36 strips of bacon

Pickling Solution

(The modern way to enjoy this dish)
2 cups of sunflower seed oil
1/2 cup of soya sauce
1/4 cup of sweet tomato sauce
1/2 cup of lemon juice
1/2 cup of wine vinegar
2 tablespoons of maple sugar
1 tablespoon of freshly ground pepper
1 teaspoon of fennel
6 tablespoons of fresh apple juice

a) Pickle seafood and vegetables for 4 hours before grilling; make a good fire.

b) Wrap each piece of seafood in a bacon strip and place on cedar sticks (6), two items of everything on each stick.
c) Grill for 10 minutes on each side. Serve on a bed of wild rice, with thyme or wild mint.

Makes six servings.

SHRIMPS ON CEDAR STICKS

2 pounds of uncooked shrimps
1 pound of bacon
40 ounces of oysters
8 cedar sticks (14 inches long)

Oyster-dipping Solution

3/4 cup of corn meal
4 tablespoons of crushed wild onions
3/4 cup of corn meal (plus a second measure)
4 tablespoons of Parmesan cheese

a) Wait until charcoal is covered with white ashes.
b) Clean shrimps by taking out the central back vein.
c) Cut bacon strips in two.
d) Cut two square pieces of aluminum foil (15 inches).
e) On one of the sheets of foil paper, mix the first measure of corn meal with the crushed wild onions. On the second sheet of foil paper, mix the second corn meal measure and cheese.
f) Roll half of the oysters in one mixture and the other half in the second mixture.
g) Roll in bacon strips.

h) On the cedar sticks, arrange alternately the wild onion oysters, cheese oysters and shrimps.
i) Grill on charcoal until golden and crispy.

Makes eight servings.

GRILLED LOBSTER

4   1 1/2 to 2-pound lobsters
1   pound of butter
3   cloves of garlic
4   teaspoons of sea salt
1/2 cup of dried watercress
1/2 teaspoon of freshly ground pepper
3   tablespoons of wild onions plus the lower part of tops
1   teaspoon of thyme
2/3 cup of lemon juice
lemon slices to taste

a) Let charcoal become grey.
b) To dress the lobsters, place each on its back and insert pointed sharp knife between tail and body through the shell.
c) Remove stomach, just behind the head, and the main gut vein from the stomach to the tail.
d) Do not remove the grey liver, as it is the most delicious part of the lobster.
e) Break the nippers.
f) Mix melted butter with crushed garlic and other ingredients, except lemon slices.

g) Roll lobsters in the sauce, and place on grill, meat facing fire, 3 inches from charcoal.
h) Cook 12 to 15 minutes to brown the meat.
i) Keep the buttered sauce hot.
j) Serve on maple or cedar boards.
k) Sprinkle with sauce.

Makes four servings.

SEAFOOD OVER AN OPEN FIRE

If you are vacationing near the sea. . .
Micmac style seashore party

---

    4 dozen round clams
    5 partridges or 5 small chickens
   10 pounds of halibut or walleye
   10 pounds of potatoes
    4 dozen ears of corn
   20 small lobsters
    1 pound of melted butter

While you wait for the meal to cook, you can serve your guests with. . .
   20 tomatoes
    1 bushel of steamed clams

If you want to stuff the clams, you need. . .
    2 loaves of bread, toasted and crumbled
    2 eggs
    6 wild onions or 12 shallots
       some sea salt
       pepper
    1 teaspoon of thyme
    1 1/2 cups of water

Select a flat area where there is no danger of setting fire to the whole forest. Make a round fire of approximately 5 feet in diameter, placing stones all around. Light a good fire in the center of these stones and let it burn for 2 hours. Have all ingredients ready, because speed is the most important part of this preparation.

If you stuff the clams, put the seafood clams on top of the stuffed mixture. Cut partridges or chickens in four and wrap them loosely in aluminum foil. Do the same to the fish.

Wash and scrub the potatoes, and husk the corn, leaving on 4 rows of the yellow husk. Wrap well but loosely in aluminum foil.

All these ingredients must be cooked in hot ashes.

If you have deep frying baskets you can use them. Put the ingredients individually into the baskets.

When all the ingredients are in the hot ashes you can cover the fire embers with seaweed to produce moisture. If you're not near the sea, use soaked burlap to cover the fire embers. You can place stones over the seaweed or burlap bags.

It usually takes 2 hours to cook this way.

Note: The fire must be at least 18 inches deep to cook properly. This meal will satisfy twenty hungry people.

POTATOES

Potatoes cook well in hot ashes or in fire embers, and they don't have to be wrapped. Simply soak them in water and drop them in the fire. The inside will be perfectly cooked, even if the peel is burnt.

CORN

If you take off the outer husk on corn, you will also be able to cook it in the hot ashes and fire embers without damaging the tender yellow grains. Fifteen minutes will be sufficient to cook it.
Butter is excellent on "corn on the cob" — a vegetable we've taught the whole world to grow and enjoy eating.

BEAVER TAIL

This is one of the Algonquin delicacies when roasted in the flames or on charcoal. Well done and crusty, although a bit fatty, it can help a tired man to regain strength even after walking twenty miles. Along with moose nose and the guts from the bull moose, it is a great specialty dish in the Algonquin culture.

HURON SAGAMITE, ASSINIWI STYLE

4 pounds of trout meat, cut in big pieces
4 pounds of moose meat, cut in 1 1/4 inch cubes (beef can replace moose)
3 pounds of beaver meat, cut in 2 inch cubes (lean pork can replace beaver)
2 pounds of red kidney beans (soaked for 12 hours)
2 pounds of hominy corn
8 wild onions or 12 shallots, finely minced
1/2 cup of maple sugar
vegetable salt and pepper to taste

a) Mix all ingredients in a cast iron pot.
b) Cover with water and cook over an open fire, well covered, for 12 to 18 hours.

HURON SAGAMITE

In the style of Mrs. Rolande Lacoste of Saint-Hubert Comté, Chambly, Quebec

---

    4   pounds of lamb roast, cut in 2 inch cubes
    4   pounds of leg of veal or beef, cut in 1 inch cubes
    3   pounds of lard (lean) cut in 2 inch cubes
    2   pounds of brown beans, washed and soaked for 12 hours
    2   pounds of hominy corn

a) Mix all ingredients and place in a cast iron pot.
b) Cover with water, add salt and pepper to taste and cover it well.
c) Cook in oven at 350°F for 10 hours or over an open fire for 15 hours.

Notes

Notes

Notes

Notes

Notes

Notes

Notes

No. 143600

1 2 3 4 5 6 7

78 77 76 75 74 73 72